How to Profit
from Bible Reading

How to Profit from Bible Reading

by

Irving L. Jensen

MOODY PRESS
CHICAGO

Except where indicated otherwise, all Scripture references in this book are from the *New American Standard Bible,* © 1960, 1962, 1963, 1968, 1971, 1972, 1973, 1975, and 1977 by the Lockman Foundation, and are used by permission.

The author wishes to thank the Lockman Foundation and also the following publishers for granting permission to use certain selections in this book:

Here's Life Publishers: Talking texts from DO-IT-YOUR-SELF Bible Studies—*Mark* (1983), *Romans* (1983).

Thomas Nelson, Inc., Publishers: *The New King James Version.* © 1979, 1980, and 1982.

Zondervan Bible Publishers: Scriptures from the HOLY BIBLE: NEW INTERNATIONAL VERSION. Copyright © 1973, 1978 by the International Society.

The use of selected references from various versions of the Bible in this publication does not necessarily imply publisher endorsement of the versions in their entirety.

Library of Congress Cataloging-in-Publication Data

Jensen, Irving Lester.
  How to profit from Bible reading.

  Bibliography: p.
  1. Bible—Reading.
I. Title.
BS617.J45   1985   220.6'028   85-11568
ISBN 0-8024-0460-X (pbk.)

1 2 3 4 5 6 7 Printing/LC/Year 88 87 86 85

Printed in the United States of America

Contents

Preface

Have you ever read an entire page in a book or magazine unaware of what you were reading? If so, you know that it is possible to *read without having read!* This book was written to help you read a passage or book of the Bible and come away feeling that you saw much of what the writer intended you to see and learn.

Bible reading is just what the two words say it is. It is not talking about the Bible, or teaching or preaching it, as important as those are. In the words of the Bible scholar Richard Moulton, "There is yet one thing left to do with the Bible: *simply to read it.*"

There are different ways to read the Bible depending on the passage chosen and the goals you have. I think there are only three basic kinds of reading. In this book I have tried to describe them in a practical way, so that you can pick up many of the suggestions and become a better Bible reader.

My thanks go to Moody Press for the invitation to write this book—the original letter said, "Someday someone needs to write a book for us on the topic 'How to read the Bible with more profit.'" And there is no way to put into words how indebted I am to my wife, Charlotte, and our children—Donna, Karen, and Bob—for their love, inspiration, and support in this and other writing endeavors.

Introduction

God has written only one book—the Bible. Of the several million books ever written, it alone deserves the name *The Book*. It should be no surprise to us that this book continues to be the most read book in the history of the world. People of all lands and languages sense a natural attraction toward it. What a priceless privilege and opportunity to read what God has written to us!

The Bible is such a large book. It is really a library of 66 books, written under divine inspiration (2 Timothy 3:16) by about 39 human authors, over a period of 1,500 years. During the years that followed, the separate books grew into one volume, the Book. In one English translation the Bible contains 773,693 words, 31,102 verses, and 1,189 chapters. The invitation and challenge to read such a large book may seem impossible to fulfill, but it should encourage us to realize that Bible reading and study are designed to last a lifetime.

Two respected modern writers have made some very remarkable observations and evaluations of books in the world today.[1] Of the several million books written in the western tradition, most of which are for amusement or mere information, they rate about 1,000 as books of enduring worth, because the books focus on how to live and are worth reading analytically. They narrow this list down to about 200 "truly great books," each one bearing these marks to the reader: (1) it is inexhaustible, (2) you see new things each time you read it, (3) it will always remain above you, (4) it will keep on lifting you till you die, (5) it will help you to grow. In their words, "These are the works that everyone should make a special effort to seek out. They are the truly great books; they are the books that anyone should choose to take with him to his own desert island."[2] It is significant that they have included the Old Testament and New Testament as two of the "truly great books."

So the Bible, God's Book, is hailed as *the* Book of all time. But how regularly and how well is it being read? Paul D. Leedy writes of readership in general that "good readers are rare," and that the average adult "comprehends about 70% of what he has read."[3] As children of God we need to hunger and thirst for the food and water of the Word. We must discipline our use of time for the many activities that bid our participation each day. We must read the Bible, and we must grow in our understanding of it.

What Is Bible Reading?

The Bible was written to be read. An unread Bible is like food that is refused, an unopened love letter, a buried sword, a road map not studied, a gold mine not worked. It has been aptly said, "A book is a book only

---

1. Mortimer J. Adler and Charles Van Doren, *How to Read a Book*, rev. ed. (New York: Simon and Schuster, 1972), pp. 341-46.
2. Ibid., p. 347.
3. Paul D. Leedy, *Improve Your Reading* (New York: McGraw-Hill, 1956), pp. 10-11.

when it is in the hands of a reader; the rest of the time it is an artifact."

A good starting point is for all of us to admit that we should do more Bible reading, and grow in the process. If one learns to *do* by *doing*, then that should be our desire. But we may rightly ask, Just what is involved in Bible reading? One dictionary definition of *read* is "to seek to interpret the true nature or meaning of someone or something through close scrutiny."[4] Reading is carefully scrutinizing the words of the page, with a solid purpose of learning. This is illustrated by the following ad, which appeared in the *New York Times*.[5]

How to Read a Love Letter

This young man has just received his first love letter. He may have already read it three or four times, but he is just beginning. To read it as accurately as he would like, would require several dictionaries and a good deal of close work with a few experts on etymology and philology.

However, he will do all right without them.

He will ponder over the exact shade of meaning of every word, every comma. She has headed the letter "*Dear John.*" What, he asks himself, is the exact significance of those words? Did she refrain from saying "*Dearest*" because she was bashful? Would "*My Dear*" have sounded too formal? . . . Maybe she would have said "*Dear So-and-So*" to anybody!

A worried frown will now appear on his face. But it disappears as soon as he really gets to thinking about the first sentence. She certainly wouldn't have written *that* to anybody!

And so he works his way through the letter, one moment perched blissfully on a cloud, the next moment

---

4. *The American Heritage Dictionary*, 1969 ed., s.v. "read."
5. *New York Times*, 10 April 1940, p. 23. The illustration was an advertisement of Mortimer Adler's book, *How to Read a Book*. Reprinted by permission of Simon & Schuster, Inc. © 1940, 1967 by Mortimer J. Adler.

huddled miserably behind an eight-ball. It has started a hundred questions in his mind. He could quote it by heart. In fact, he will—to himself—for weeks to come.

It is interesting to see how the ad applies the illustration to reading in general:

> If people read books with anything like the same concentration, we'd be a race of mental giants. But we don't—and we aren't. And it's unlikely that even the greatest book can be read with the same intensity and devotion to detail the young man above has employed in reading his first love letter.
>
> Yet most of us could read books a lot better than we do. In fact, very few people really know how.
>
> Which is nothing to be ashamed of—we were simply not taught how in schools. We were taught only how to read words, and reading books is an altogether different thing.

The word *read* (with its cognates) appears eighty-four times in the Bible, thirty-seven of those in the New Testament. Often understanding or application are associated with the reading: "Do you understand what you are reading?" (Acts 8:30); "When you read you can understand" (Ephesians 3:4). Bible reading is not Bible study, but the two are very closely related.

Bible reading is both external and internal. The external aspect is physical—the eye viewing the page or the voice speaking and the ear hearing if the text is also being read aloud. It requires careful scrutiny and should involve repetition.

The internal experience of Bible reading is the reflection of mind and spirit as the passage is being looked at, trying to understand and respond to the message. The responses are spiritual, involving vital soul decisions such as confession of sin, faith, praise, and obedience. A young Chinese student revealed how far along he had come in his spiritual growth when he said, "I am now reading the Bible and behaving it."

Some Bible students like to mark their Bibles while they are reading, to register their inward responses. Any kind of record kept during or after reading is extremely valuable, because it enlarges the field of observation.

What Are the Values of Bible Reading?

If God wrote His Bible to be read, then the very reading must be exceedingly and eternally valuable. Paul encouraged Timothy to keep on reading the God-inspired Scriptures, because that was the source of Timothy's wisdom that led to his "salvation through faith which is in Christ Jesus" (2 Timothy 3:15). Besides that, it would make him thoroughly "equipped for every good work" as a man of God, the Word being "profit-able for teaching, for reproof, for correction, for train-ing in righteousness" (2 Timothy 3:16). The word *profit-able* translates a Greek word whose root is *increase*. Reading God's Word can make you *increase* and grow and mature in your Christian life, making you more and more like your Master. Hence the title of this book, *How to Profit from Bible Reading.*

Such are the eternal benefits of Bible reading. But we can't overlook the immediate enjoyment and excite-ment of reading this great Book. If you are in tune with the divine Author as you read it, you can understand the emotions of men like David and Paul: "O how I love Thy law! It is my meditation all the day" (Psalm 119:97); "Oh, the depth of the riches both of the wisdom and knowledge of God!" (Romans 11:33).

And there are hosts of other values of Bible read-ing, some of which will come to light as we move along in this volume. Read all of Psalm 119 and you will learn many of the blessings that David traced to the reading of God's Word.

1

The Setting of Bible Reading

This is a "how to" book, about methods of reading the Bible for lasting profit and full enjoyment. In this chapter we will find answers to Who, What, Why, Where, and When concerning Bible reading and will learn the three basic kinds of reading. The second chapter will show us How to get ready for Bible reading, and in the last three chapters the three kinds of reading will be described and illustrated.

For the most part, references in this book to Bible reading will not be of long parts of the Bible but of short passages, such as a chapter or paragraph.

I. Who Are the Readers?

Everyone should read the Bible, regardless of background, heritage, race, position, age, education, or even spiritual relationship to God. The individual books were written for particular groups or individuals in the original settings, but they came together as a universal volume, to be read by all—believers *and* unbelievers.

A. UNBELIEVERS

Among unbelievers who read the Bible are those who are genuine seekers of truth and those who are merely curious. All unbelievers need to read the Bible—in fact, the Bible is the key evangelistic witness of salvation to lost souls. This is the major objective of the distribution of the new Bible edition called *The Book*, as seen in this challenge appearing on its first page: "We challenge you. Read *The Book*—it could be the most important and life-changing step you will ever take."[1]

B. BELIEVERS

Most serious, regular Bible readers are Christians, those who have experienced new birth and have new life in Christ. Their knowledge of the Word led them to Christ through the Spirit's ministry, and now the Word has become their daily spiritual food and trustworthy guide. Three groups can be identified in the category of believers:

1) Newborn babes in Christ, just converted. Their enthusiasm in the Scriptures is boundless and heartening.
2) Active, growing, mature believers, of young and middle age. From this group come most of the local church's lay and professional workers.
3) Older believers, still maturing. These are the spiritual elders in the wide sense (men and women), who continue to read the Bible and find that it remains fruitful and inexhaustible.

If you are an earnest Christian reader it is *you* who can adequately understand the Bible. That is because of your relationship to your heavenly Father. Because you

1. *The Book*, a special edition of *The Living Bible* (Wheaton, Ill.: Tyndale, 1984), p. 1.

love Him, you want to grow in your knowledge of Him and your understanding of what He has written in His Book. It was not always that way. Your change of heart made the difference. The believer has a new heart (1 Corinthians 2:14); a hungry heart (1 Peter 2:2); an obedient heart (Jeremiah 7:23); a disciplined heart (Proverbs 23:12); and a teachable heart (Isaiah 50:4).[2] And the Holy Spirit, who inspired the Scriptures, dwells within your heart, teaching and guiding you (John 14:26; 16:13).

II. What Is the Bible?

Some things stand or fall together. If our hearts are dull, our reading is dull. If we regard the Bible as just another book, our reading is just another exercise. Let's spend some time focusing on what the Bible really is.

A. IT IS A BOOK

The first thing to recognize about the Bible is that it is a book with a unified theme. (The theme is God's salvation to sinful man by Jesus Christ.) The Bible is also a library of sixty-six volumes that came together through the course of several centuries by the guiding hand of God. Thirty-nine were written before Christ and are called the Old Testament; twenty-seven were written after Christ and are now referred to as the New Testament. These divine volumes are works of literature, to be read as such. There are prose writings, such as the many historical books, and there are poetical books, such as the Psalms. When we are reading prose, we can expect to see plain language recounting the truth. The epistles of the New Testament have their own unique characteristics, and we read them as personal letters revealing the great truths of God and of practi-

2. T. Norton Sterrett, *How to Understand Your Bible* (Downers Grove, Ill.: InterVarsity, 1977), pp. 19-22.

cal Christian living. When we are reading poetry, we can expect to see much figurative language, presenting the truth in another way. The human authors of the books of the Bible followed normal grammatical and compositional rules and procedures as they wrote under the moving hand of the Spirit.

The format of a book of the Bible is also like any other book. There are chapters, which are broken down into paragraphs, then sentences (usually the length of a verse), then words. All Bibles now follow a standard system of chapter divisions (originated by Stephen Langton in 1228) and verse divisions (originated by Robert Stephanus in 1560). Paragraph divisions have never been standardized, but the paragraph units shown in your Bible should be kept in mind when you read the text. Most modern versions show paragraph divisions by means of some printing device such as indentation, asterisk, or bold type.

Though there is a general chronological order in the arrangement of the sixty-six books (from the original creation, Genesis, to the new creation, Revelation), the books were placed in their present order according to general topics and types of groups. Observe on the charts (figs. 1.1 and 1.2) how the books are grouped in each of the two Testaments. The numbers at the top of each chart indicate how many books are in each group.

Books of the Old Testament

5	12	5	5	12
PENTATEUCH	HISTORY	POETRY	MAJOR PROPHETS	MINOR PROPHETS
Genesis to Deuteronomy	Joshua to Esther	Job to Songs	Isaiah to Lamentations	Hosea to Malachi
Mainly Narrative		Mainly Reflection	Mainly Oracles	

Fig. 1.1

Books of the New Testament

5	21	1
HISTORY	LETTERS	PROPHECY
4 Gospels Acts	13 Pauline Epistles 8 General Epistles	Revelation
Mainly Narrative	Mainly Interpretation	Mainly Prophecy

Fig. 1.2

B. IT IS A UNIQUE BOOK

When you read the Bible you are reading a book, but it is a unique book. Someone has said, "Treat the Bible like any other book and you will find that it is not like any other book." The world has never seen a book like the Bible. Both its history and content bear this out.

1. *Its unique history.* No book has come into being like the Bible. It originated by God's breath—"all Scripture is inspired by God [God-breathed]" (2 Timothy 3:16). The human authors spoke from God as they were borne along by the Holy Spirit—"men spoke from God as they were carried along by the Holy Spirit" (2 Peter 1:21, NIV*).

The Bible is a miracle in that its sixty-six individual books gradually *grew* into one unit, called the canon. F. F. Bruce says, "The Bible is not simply an anthology; there is a unity which binds the whole together."[3]

The Bible cannot be matched as to (1) its transmission through thousands of ancient scribal copyings; (2) its very survival through all kinds of attacks to destroy it; and (3) its worldwide reception and influence.

*New International Version.

3. F. F. Bruce, *The Books and the Parchments*, rev. ed. (Old Tappan, N.J.: Revell, 1984), p. 79.

2. *Its unique content.* The Bible is God's only written communication to us. As we read it, we learn that God *wants* to save us from the guilt of sin and that He *can* save us.

The Bible is completely trustworthy. The absolute Word of the absolute God is absolute authority for life. If God cannot be trusted, who can?

Further, the Bible is uniquely inexhaustible. Every time you read the Bible you will find new things to think about. Here is how Augustine expressed it, in writing his son in A.D. 412: "Such is the depth of the Christian Scriptures that even if I were attempting to study them and nothing else from early boyhood to decrepit old age, with the utmost leisure, the most unwearied zeal, and talents greater than I have, I would still daily be making progress in discovering their treasures."

C. IT IS GOD'S MESSAGE TO US

Much of the Bible reads like a history book. About 70 percent of the Old Testament and 60 percent of the New Testament are narrative. God chose to reveal Himself that way. One of the important things to recognize about the two Testaments is that together they comprise *one* book. The New Testament did not supersede or cancel the Old Testament. That is confirmed by Jesus and His apostles, who often cited the Old Testament by using the present tense (e.g., "he says" rather than "he said" in Matthew 13:14). Figure 1.3 shows the intimate relationships of the two Testaments, including the historical connections.

When you are reading an Old Testament book, you are in the basic section of the pyramid, involving the necessary historical foundations. Old Testament books are also picture books, filled with symbols, types, and narratives illustrating the great theological truths enacted and expounded in the New. Also throughout the

Old are the many prophetical anticipations of the New. So the Old Testament supports, enlightens, and anticipates the New, causing the peak of divine revelation—God speaking in His Son (Hebrews 1:1-2)—to rise high in all of its glory.

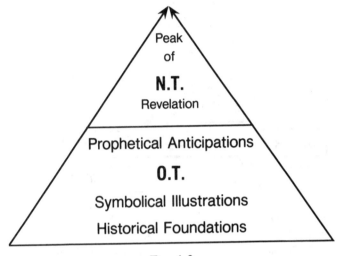

Peak
of

N.T.
Revelation

Prophetical Anticipations

O.T.

Symbolical Illustrations

Historical Foundations

Fig. 1.3

God's Book has three main objectives, which you will observe as you read its pages:

1) Revelation—to uncover His person and work, and diagnose man's heart
2) Redemption—to bring sinful man to Himself
3) Instruction—to help the redeemed person to live pleasing to Him

Every passage of the Bible, whether in the Old or New Testament, has something to say about one or more of these universal subjects (fig. 1.4):

When you read a passage, look for these truths. It will amaze you how much you will find. The main thread throughout the Bible is that of *salvation* (right

side of the diagram, fig. 1.4). Whether you are in the
Old or New Testament, you will find the bringer of
salvation, the way of salvation, and the people of salvation (believers) to be the same.

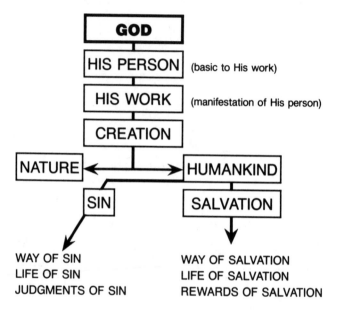

Fig. 1.4

When you are about to read a Bible passage, it will
help you to have identified already the passage in the
time-line of history, so that you are aware of what you
may *expect* to see in the text, at least in a general way.
For example, if you are reading in the Old Testament,
you can expect that the passage has some reference to
Israel, since that nation is the main subject from Genesis
12 on. Suppose you are reading in Acts (New Testament)—you see that Jesus has ascended to heaven, and
you may rightly ask, "Now what?"

The chart in figure 1.5 will help you make those
connections before you read a passage. (The last Old
Testament book, Malachi, was written around 400 B.C.,

and the last New Testament book, Revelation, was written around A.D. 100.) Note: The entry God and His Universal Redemptive Plan reminds us that all Bible narratives reveal something of God's plan, whether or not Israel or the church is part of the narrative.[4]

BIBLE CONTENT AND WORLD HISTORY

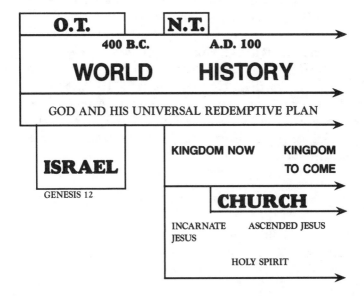

Fig. 1.5

III. Why Read the Bible?

It is important to ask this question because *why* we want to read the Bible determines *how* we will read it.[5] And everyone *does* have reasons for reading. I. A. Richards writes,

> We always read for some purpose—unless some sad, bad, mad schoolteacher has got hold of us. There is no such

---

4. See Gordon D. Fee and Douglas Stuart, *How to Read the Bible for All Its Worth* (Grand Rapids: Zondervan, 1982), pp. 74-75.
5. Psalm 119 has much to say about the purpose of Bible reading.

thing as merely reading words; always through the words we are trafficking or trying to traffic with things—things gone by, present, to come or eternal.[6]

A. GOD HAS SPOKEN TO US

It is *God* who has spoken, and what a great God He is! His Book is a call to a complete trust and worship. As one writer says, "We read the Bible uncritically, for we hold that what it says, God says, and *who are we to teach God!*"[7] The first major truth recorded by the writer of Hebrews was that "God has spoken" (1:1-2), and this was followed by the warning, "We must pay much closer attention to what we have heard" (2:1). The writer could just as well have used the words *written* and *read* in these verses.

B. WE NEED TO KNOW WHAT HE HAS SAID

God didn't write the Scriptures as a pastime. It was His way of sending us a life-and-death message with eternal dimensions. He had some things He wanted us to know. We are His creatures, and we must read His Book and respond to it.

Our reading is not only to gain more information; it is to understand more than we understood before the reading. And with that enlightenment comes the enjoyment of hearing God's voice through the written Word.

When we read the Bible we are learning what life is all about. God tells us where we came from—the origins of the *past*. Bruce Waltke says that "the Old Testament is a lens that enables us to view life with 20/20 vision. Without it we would be in the dark regarding the great-

---

6. I. A. Richards, *How to Read a Page* (Boston: Beacon, 1942), p. 20.
7. James W. Sire, *How to Read Slowly: A Christian Guide* (Downers Grove, Ill.: InterVarsity, 1978), p. 147. Emphasis added.

er questions of life—our origin and reason for being."[8] The New Testament gives the same kinds of answers. God in His Word tells us why we are here: to come to the eternal life of faith, today, which is the *present*. And He reveals where we are going, depending on our response to His present invitations. That is the *future*, recorded in forms of promise, warning, and prophecy.

As believers we need to read the Bible for spiritual growth—"Thy word I have treasured in my heart, that I may not sin against Thee" (Psalm 119:11); for instruction of doctrine—"But regarding the resurrection of the dead, have you not read that which was spoken to you by God?" (Matthew 22:31); and for help in ministering to others—"Let the word of Christ richly dwell within you . . . teaching and admonishing one another" (Colossians 3:16).

Salvation is the key subject of all of the Bible, so the Savior, Jesus Christ, is its key person. He appears in the opening verses of the Book (Genesis 1:1; cf. John 1:1-3; 1 John 1:1-3), and in the closing verses He promises to return to earth (Revelation 22:20-21). All the pages in between point to Jesus. We need to know what God has said in His Book about His Son. John R. W. Stott writes of this:

> It seems to me that our greatest need today is an enlarged vision of Jesus Christ. We need to see Him as the One in whom alone the fulness of God dwells and in whom alone we can come to fulness of life (Colossians 1:19; 2:9, 10).
>   There is only one way to gain clear, true, fresh, lofty views of Christ, and that is through the Bible. The Bible is the prism by which the light of Jesus Christ is broken into its many and beautiful colours. The Bible is the portrait of Jesus Christ. We need to gaze upon Him with

8. Bruce Waltke, "Why Read the Old Testament?" *Moody Monthly,* February 1984, p. 46.

such intensity of desire that (by the gracious work of the Holy Spirit) He comes alive to us, meets with us, and fills us with Himself.[9]

IV. When and Where to Read the Bible

These practical areas may seem unimportant, but they focus on some things that can help or mar an effective program of Bible reading for you. This is because reading is something that is *done*, and time and place are always involved in an activity or practice.

Be willing to spend time—that precious commodity—in reading the Bible. A. W. Tozer once said, "God has not bowed to our nervous haste nor embraced the methods of our machine age. The man who will know God must give time to Him." Our priorities are the key, as James W. Sire writes, "If you can find time to do anything other than stay alive, you can find time for reading. . . . It's all a matter of determining priorities, deciding what you *should* do with the twenty-four hours God gives all of us each day."[10]

How much do you value having *extended* times for studying the Bible? National Geographic magazine tells a moving story about 81-year-old Carl Sharsmith, veteran park ranger in California's Yosemite National Park, one of the world's best-loved national parks:

Carl was back at his tent quarters after a long afternoon with tourists. His nose was flaked white and red with sunburn; his eyes were watery, partly from age but also from disappointment at hearing again an *old question* after a half century of summers in California's Yosemite National Park.

A lady tourist had hit him with a question where it hurt: "I've only got an hour to spend at Yosemite," she

9. John R. W. Stott, *Understanding the Bible* (Glendale, Calif.: Regal, 1972), pp. 8-9.
10. Sire, p. 152.

declared. "What should I do? Where should I go?"

The old naturalist-interpreter-ranger finally found the voice to reply:

"Ah, lady. Only an hour." He repeated it slowly. "I suppose if I had only an hour to spend at Yosemite, I'd just walk over there by the river and *sit down and cry*."[11]

We would do well to reflect on that last line and apply it to our attitude toward Bible study.

A. WHEN?

Whatever pattern of reading you follow, it should fit your needs, abilities, setting, and interests. There is no such thing as one pattern for all. Here are some suggestions for you to consider.

- Follow a regular, consistent pattern as much as possible. This guards your reading against intrusion by things that pop up unexpectedly.
- Read at least once each day, more frequently if possible (Psalm 1:2-3; Colossians 1:9). You don't have to ask God, "Should I read the Bible today, Lord?" The length of reading may be short or long. Variety is good.
- Devotional reading should be done when the setting is quiet, without distractions.
- Your reading may be part of a Bible study project, which may involve scheduled times.
- Choose the time of day when you are most alert, wide awake, least rushed, and can concentrate the best. This time varies from person to person. Some like to read in the freshness of the early morning hours, others are their best when evening comes, and for others the noon hour is most productive.

11. David S. Boyer, "Yosemite—Forever?" *National Geographic*, January 1985, p. 55.

As noted earlier, the key to scheduling time for Bible reading lies in setting priorities. Don't let other things (as good as they may be of themselves) squeeze out Bible reading. Sire warns about the pitfall of mixed-up priorities:

> That which pulls on me at the moment gets my attention, and I tend to let the more important long-range goals take a back seat to less important immediate demands. . . . Our task before God is to learn his general will for our lives and to make decisions regarding our use of time within that framework.[12]

B. WHERE?

Most Bible reading is done alone, because for the most part it is the personal devotion and search of each child of God, face to face with his Lord. Choose a place for reading that will help to keep you alert. There shouldn't be distractions; the lighting, ventilation, and temperature should be comfortable. The less you are aware of your surroundings while reading, the better. It will be helpful to use a desk or table, especially if you extend your reading to the valuable habit of recording things on paper.

If you are reading with others, the group or occasion determines the location, for example, in a church, classroom, or home.

V. Different Kinds of Bible Reading

Notice that these pages are about different *kinds*, not *levels* of reading (for example, levels from beginners to experienced readers). Adler and Van Doren say there are four levels of reading a book: (1) elementary reading—the basic reading for beginners, not going beyond what the text says; (2) inspectional reading—a systematic skimming of the whole book, trying to conclude what

12. Ibid., p. 154.

the whole book is about; (3) analytical reading—thorough reading, "chewing and digesting" the book, preeminently for the sake of understanding; (4) syn-topical reading—the difficult comparative study of various books around one subject.[13]

So there are levels of reading, in degrees of difficulty. But here we are looking at *kinds* of reading, the kinds being determined by the purposes of the readings. You don't read the Bible just for the sake of looking at a printed text. You read with a purpose. In this book we are looking at the *practical* ways of reading by the average Christian layman. There are three kinds, representing three different purposes. They can be identified by three logograms (fig. 1.6).

Kinds of Bible Reading

 devotional → READ TO WORSHIP

 analytical → READ TO ANALYZE

⁻,⁻,⁻, informational → READ TO BE INFORMED

Fig. 1.6

All three of these involve Bible passages of practical, short-to-moderate lengths. Two special kinds of reading (not included here) are (1) the survey (synthetic) reading of a whole book, and (2) the comparison of words and phrases throughout the Bible (comparative or topical reading).

A. DEVOTIONAL READING

Devotional reading is done especially in doctrinal passages (e.g., Pauline epistles), but it is not restricted to

13. Adler and Van Doren, pp. 16-20.

those. For example, excellent passages for devotional reading may be found in prayers, testimonies, and narratives (e.g., the life of Jesus).

The purposes of devotional reading are spiritual inspiration and challenge for practical application. Note on the diagram that in devotional reading you read to worship. This does not mean that worship is excluded from the other kinds of reading, but that it is the prevailing experience of the person in devotional reading.

The triangle logogram points to the worship aspect of devotional reading, suggesting among other things the unity and trinity of the Godhead.

B. ANALYTICAL READING

Analytical reading is slower, usually done with the intention of multiple readings to follow, as compared with informational reading, in which a passage is usually read once. Analytical reading is done in units of segments, paragraphs, and verses.

The underlying purpose of analytical reading is to fully observe the Bible text as a basis for interpreting and applying it.

The rectangle logogram points to a segment as a unit of Bible reading, divided into paragraphs. This rectangle shows three paragraphs.

C. INFORMATIONAL READING ⁻,⁻,⁻,

Informational reading is done mainly in the historical narratives of the Bible, of which there are many. It picks up the many facts of the text to construct the picture that is intended by the writer.

The purpose of informational reading is to gather knowledge of the Bible's history and subjects related to it, with practical applications in view. "These things happened to them as an example, and they were written for our instruction" (1 Corinthians 10:11a).

The logogram of successive lines points to the accumulating progression of many recorded facts and subjects which are the objects of informational reading.

Very closely related to informational reading is what may be called *occasional* reading. This is reading done for special occasions, such as weddings, funerals, graduations, dedications, and holidays.

2

Preparation for Bible Reading

The process of reading, as we are learning in this book, is not the mere picking up the Bible, having hasty eye contact with a passage, and putting the Bible down. Rather, it involves:

1) Getting ready to read
2) Doing the reading and even repeated readings
3) Reflecting on the reading afterward and possibly recording on paper

What is involved in getting ready to read? Some preparations are permanent, once they are made, such as the gathering of tools and equipment. A second kind of preparation is always conditional, depending on you, the reader. The third kind involves checks that should always be made before reading a passage. Let's look at each kind of preparation.

I. Tools and Equipment

Good craftsmen use good tools and always keep them in good condition. How much thought have you

Two-Column Bible Text

Jude 1-25 (NASB)[1]

The Warnings of History to the Ungodly

1 JUDE, a bond-servant of Jesus Christ, and brother of 2James, to cthose who are the called, beloved in God the Father, and dkept for Jesus Christ:

2 aMay mercy and peace and love bbe multiplied to you.

3 aBeloved, while I was making every effort to write you about our bcommon salvation, I felt the necessity to write to you appealing that you ccontend earnestly for dthe faith which was once for all edelivered to fthe 1saints.

4 For certain persons have acrept in unnoticed, those who were long beforehand 1bmarked out for this condemnation, ungodly persons who turn cthe grace of our God into dlicentiousness and edeny our only Master and Lord, Jesus Christ.

5 Now I desire to aremind you, though byou know all things once for all, that 1the Lord, cafter saving a people out of the land of Egypt, 2subsequently destroyed those who did not believe.

6 And angels who did not keep their own domain, but abandoned their proper abode, He has bkept in eternal bonds under darkness for the judgment of the great day.

7 Just as aSodom and Gomorrah and the bcities around them, since they in the same way as these indulged in gross immorality, and cwent after strange flesh, are exhibited as an 1dexample, in undergoing the epunishment of eternal fire.

8 Yet in the same manner these men, also by dreaming, adefile the flesh, and reject authority, and revile 1angelic majesties.

9 But aMichael bthe archangel, when he disputed with the devil and argued about cthe body of Moses, did not dare pronounce against him a railing judgment, but said, "dThe Lord rebuke you."

10 But athese men revile the things which they do not understand; and bthe things which they know by instinct, alike unreasoning animals, by these things they are 1destroyed.

11 Woe to them! For they have gone athe way of Cain, and for pay 1they have rushed headlong into bthe error of Balaam, and cperished in the rebellion of Korah.

12 These men are those who are 1hidden reefs ain your love feasts when they feast with you bwithout fear, caring for themselves; cclouds without water, dcarried along by winds; autumn trees without fruit, 2doubly dead, euprooted;

13 awild waves of the sea, casting up btheir own 1shame like foam; wandering stars, cfor whom the 2black darkness has been reserved forever.

14 And about these also aEnoch, *in* the seventh *generation* from Adam, prophesied, saying, "bBehold, the Lord came with 1many thousands of His holy ones,

15 ato execute judgment upon all, and to convict all the ungodly of all their ungodly deeds which they have done in an ungodly way, and of all the harsh things which bungodly sinners have spoken against Him."

16 These are agrumblers, finding fault, bfollowing after their *own* lusts; 1they speak carrogantly, flattering people dfor the sake of *gaining* an advantage.

Keep Yourselves in the Love of God

17 But you, abeloved, bought to remember the words that were spoken beforehand by cthe apostles of our Lord Jesus Christ,

18 that they were saying to you, "aIn the last time there shall be mockers, bfollowing after their own ungodly lusts."

19 These are the ones who cause divisions, 1aworldly-minded, 2devoid of the Spirit.

20 But you, abeloved, bbuilding yourselves up on your most holy afaith; cpraying in the Holy Spirit;

21 keep yourselves in the love of God, awaiting anxiously for the mercy of our Lord Jesus Christ to eternal life.

22 And 1have mercy on some, who are doubting;

23 save others, asnatching them out of the fire; and on some have mercy with fear, bhating even the garment polluted by the flesh.

24 aNow to Him who is able to keep you from stumbling, and to bmake you stand in the presence of His glory blameless with cgreat joy,

25 to the aonly bGod our Savior, through Jesus Christ our Lord, cbe glory, majesty, dominion and authority, dbefore all time and now and 1forever. Amen.

Center-column references:

1 1Gr., *Judas* 2Or, *Jacob*
aMatt. 13:55; Mark 6:3; [Luke 6:16; John 14:22; Acts 1:13?] bRom. 1:1 cRom. 1:6f. dJohn 17:11f.; 1 Pet. 1:5; Jude 21
2 aGal. 6:16; 1 Tim. 1:2 b1 Pet. 1:2; 2 Pet. 1:2
3 1Or, *holy ones* aRom. 6:9; Jude 1, 17, 20 bTitus 1:4 c1 Tim. 6:12 dActs 6:7; Jude 20 e2 Pet. 2:21 fActs 9:13
4 1Or, *written about* aGal. 2:4; 2 Tim. 3:6 b1 Pet. 2:8 cActs 11:23 d2 Pet. 2:7 e2 Tim. 2:12; Titus 1:16; 2 Pet. 2:1; 1 John 2:22
5 1Some ancient mss. read *Jesus* 2Lit., *the second time* a2 Pet. 1:12f.; 3:1f. b1 John 2:20 cEx. 12:51; 1 Cor. 10:5-10; Heb. 3:16f.
6 a2 Pet. 2:4 b2 Pet. 2:9
7 1Or, *example of eternal fire, in undergoing punishment* aGen. 19:24f.; 2 Pet. 2:6 bDeut. 29:23; Hos. 11:8 c2 Pet. 2:2 d2 Pet. 2:6 eMatt. 25:41; 2 Thess. 1:8f.; 2 Pet. 3:7
8 1Lit., *glories* a2 Pet. 2:10
9 aDan. 10:13, 21; 12:1; Rev. 12:7 b1 Thess. 4:16; 2 Pet. 2:11 cDeut. 34:6 dZech. 3:2
10 1Lit., *corrupted* a2 Pet. 2:12 bPhil. 3:19
11 1Lit., *they have poured themselves out* aGen. 4:3-8; Heb. 11:4; 1 John 3:12 bNum. 31:16; 2 Pet. 2:15; Rev. 2:14 cNum. 16:1-3, 31-35
12 1Or, *stains* 2Lit., *twice* a1 Cor. 11:20ff.; 2 Pet. 2:13 and mg. bEzek. 34:2, 8, 10 cProv. 25:14; 2 Pet. 2:17 dEph. 4:14 eMatt. 15:13
13 1Or, *shameless deeds* 2Lit., *blackness of darkness*; or, *nether gloom* aIs. 57:20 bPhil. 3:19 c2 Pet. 2:17; Jude 6
14 1Lit., *His holy ten thousands* aGen. 5:18, 21ff. bDeut. 33:2; Dan. 7:10; Matt. 16:27; Heb. 12:22
15 a2 Pet. 2:6ff.
16 1Lit., *their mouth speaks* aNum. 16:11, 41; 1 Cor. 10:10 b2 Pet. 2:10; Jude 18 c2 Pet. 2:18 d2 Pet. 2:3
17 aJude 3 b2 Pet. 3:2 cHeb. 2:3
18 aActs 20:29; 1 Tim. 4:1; 2 Tim. 3:1f.; 4:3; 2 Pet. 3:3 bJude 4, 16
19 1Or, *merely natural* 2Lit., *not having* a1 Cor. 2:14f.; James 3:15
20 aJude 3 bCol. 2:7; 1 Thess. 5:11 cEph. 6:18
21 aTitus 2:13; Heb. 9:28; 2 Pet. 3:12
22 1Some ancient mss. read *convince*
23 aAmos 4:11; Zech. 3:2; 1 Cor. 3:15 bZech. 3:3f.; Rev. 3:4
24 aRom. 16:25 b2 Cor. 4:14 c1 Pet. 4:13
25 1Lit., *to all the ages* aJohn 5:44; 1 Tim. 1:17 bLuke 1:47 cRom. 11:36 dHeb. 13:8

Fig. 2.1

1. Thinline *New American Standard Reference Bible* (Chicago: Moody Press).

One-Column Bible Text

Ephesians 3:17—4:21 (NIV)

his Spirit in your inner being, [17]so that Christ may dwell in your hearts through faith. And I pray that you, being rooted and established in love, [18]may have power, together with all the saints, to grasp how wide and long and high and deep is the love of Christ, [19]and to know this love that surpasses knowledge—that you may be filled to the measure of all the fullness of God.

[20]Now to him who is able to do immeasurably more than all we ask or imagine, according to his power that is at work within us, [21]to him be glory in the church and in Christ Jesus throughout all generations, for ever and ever! Amen.

Unity in the Body of Christ

4 As a prisoner for the Lord, then, I urge you to live a life worthy of the calling you have received. [2]Be completely humble and gentle; be patient, bearing with one another in love. [3]Make every effort to keep the unity of the Spirit through the bond of peace. [4]There is one body and one Spirit—just as you were called to one hope when you were called— [5]one Lord, one faith, one baptism; [6]one God and Father of all, who is over all and through all and in all.

[7]But to each one of us grace has been given as Christ apportioned it. [8]This is why it[a] says:

> "When he ascended on high,
>   he led captives in his train
>   and gave gifts to men."[b]

[9](What does "he ascended" mean except that he also descended to the lower, earthly regions? [10]He who descended is the very one who ascended higher than all the heavens, in order to fill the whole universe.) [11]It was he who gave some to be apostles, some to be prophets, some to be evangelists, and some to be pastors and teachers, [12]to prepare God's people for works of service, so that the body of Christ may be built up [13]until we all reach unity in the faith and in the knowledge of the Son of God and become mature, attaining to the whole measure of the fullness of Christ.

[14]Then we will no longer be infants, tossed back and forth by the waves, and blown here and there by every wind of teaching and by the cunning and craftiness of men in their deceitful scheming. [15]Instead, speaking the truth in love, we will in all things grow up into him who is the Head, that is, Christ. [16]From him the whole body, joined and held together by every supporting ligament, grows and builds itself up in love, as each part does its work.

Living as Children of Light

[17]So I tell you this, and insist on it in the Lord, that you must no longer live as the Gentiles do, in the futility of their thinking. [18]They are darkened in their understanding and separated from the life of God because of the ignorance that is in them due to the hardening of their hearts. [19]Having lost all sensitivity, they have given themselves over to sensuality so as to indulge in every kind of impurity, with a continual lust for more.

[20]You, however, did not come to know Christ that way. [21]Surely

[a]8 Or *God*   [b]8 Psalm 68:18

Fig. 2.2

given to tools as having something to do with how effective your Bible reading is?

A. A GOOD EDITION OF THE BIBLE

Versions of the Bible are printed in various editions, representing a wide spectrum of format, quality, and price. You can help your personal Bible reading immeasurably by choosing the right Bible. When making your choice take the following points into consideration.

1. *Print.* Large, clear, bold print, with liberal space between lines, is ideal.

2. *Paper.* Is the paper conducive to ink or pencil notations, without bleeding to the opposite side?

3. *Columns.* One of the most obvious differences of Bibles is the format involving columns. Many editions have two columns. More and more of the newer editions are following the standard book format of one wider column. Compare the samples shown (figs. 2.1 and 2.2).

One of the shortcomings of the two-column text is that twice as many phrases are broken up at the right side of each line than are broken up in the one-column text. Occasionally, however, individual phrases stand out clearly and prominently (see the first line of Jude 21). Preservation of full phrases is important in Bible reading and study.

4. *Paragraph and verse divisions.* We were taught in school to read paragraph by paragraph, and the Bible authors wrote in paragraphical units,[2] so it is important

---

2. Our early manuscripts do not show verse, paragraph, or even chapter divisions. But the content of the writings shows that the authors composed their books with units of thought in mind, such as paragraph units.

to read and study the Bible paragraph by paragraph. Most Bibles show paragraph divisions, by such devices as indentation (NIV), bold-face verse number (NASB), or asterisk (some KJV*). The paragraph and one-column format of many editions of the *New International Version* comes closest to the standard book format with which we are familiar.

5. *Margin spaces.* Generous spaces in margins are valuable, because they allow for notations.

6. *Quotes from the Old Testament.* Old Testament quotations are an important part of the New Testament text, and their effectiveness for Bible reading depends much on how they are printed in the Bible edition. NASB uses capital letters for the entire quote, NIV sets off the quote in block form. The *Ryrie Study Bible* does both, which is the clearest.

7. *Reference notes.* These are cross-references of related Bible passages and short commentaries or notations. They appear in the margins (NASB); in a center column or at the bottom of the pages (most editions of NIV) or in side margins (Bible verses) *and* footnotes (commentary) (Ryrie Study Bible). Reference notes are used mostly for detailed Bible study, not Bible reading.

B. CHOICE OF VERSIONS

Which version of the Bible should you read? You should concentrate mostly on one version, letting its words become a part of you, as you read and meditate on them. The version you choose for this is the one about which you would say, "This is *my* Bible."

When you have read a Bible passage in one version, you should always read it in at least one other version. If

*King James Version.

the first reading is in a literal version (e.g., NKJV*), it would be good to do the other reading in a freer translation (e.g., NIV). One of the values of reading a second version is that you will see things you never saw before because of the different vocabulary and style. (Accuracy is not involved in such differences.)

Figure 2.3 contains a list of the major English Bible versions, the order of the list going from the very literal to the very paraphrastic.[3] (See also Appendix 6.) This will help you decide in what versions you want to do your Bible reading.

1. New King James Version	(NKJV, 1982)	literal
2. New American Standard Bible	(NASB, 1971)	
3. Revised Standard Version	(RSV, 1952)	translations
4. New Berkeley Version in Modern English (Modern Language Bible)	(MLB, 1959)	to
5. New International Version	(NIV, 1978)	free
6. Good News Bible (Today's English Version)	(TEV, 1976)	translations
7. New English Bible	(NEB, 1970)	to
8. Jerusalem Bible (Roman Catholic)	(JB, 1966)	
9. New Testament in Modern English (Phillips)	(Phillips, 1958)	paraphrases
10. The Living Bible	(TLB, 1971)	

Fig. 2.3

C. PENCIL, PAPER, AND NOTEBOOK

By now you are beginning to see that Bible reading in its fullest dimensions is more than mere eye contact with the printed page. Using a pencil as you read the Bible text can be one of the best aids for seeing what the author has written.

Unless you are gifted with a photographic memory, it is impossible for you to retain for very long all the things you see in a productive reading of a biblical passage. That is because the Bible contains so much and

*New King James Version.
3. See Robert Thomas, "Why All the Translations?" Christian Life, October 1978. The freer the translation, the more communicative is the objective of the translator. Literal versions aim at word-for-word translation.

because the divine activity of illumination is going on in your mind as you meditate on the Word. There is no comparable reading situation in all the world.

What can you do to retain what you see? *Jot it down!* Make note of it on a piece of paper and in the margins of your Bible. Underline words and phrases that strike fire in your soul. Record your observations as you see them, and your mind will be released to look for more. Not only does recording provide a permanent record of what you have seen in your reading, it also initiates other lines of inquiry. And when you return to that passage at a later time, you will find that the marked passage resounds like an echo of your earlier impressions and experiences with it.

Apply what Adler and Van Doren say to your own Bible reading:

> When you buy a book, you establish a property right in it, just as you do in clothes or furniture when you buy and pay for them. But the act of purchase is actually only the prelude to possession in the case of a book. Full ownership of a book only comes when you have made it a part of yourself, and the best way to make yourself a part of it—which comes to the same thing—is by writing in it.
>
> Why is marking a book indispensable to reading it? First, it keeps you awake—not merely conscious, but wide awake. Second, reading, if it is active, is thinking, and thinking tends to express itself in words, spoken or written. The person who says he knows what he thinks but cannot express it usually does not know what he thinks. Third, writing your reactions down helps you to remember the thoughts of the author.[4]

One telephone company placed the following advertisement in its phone book regarding its yellow page section. What does this say to you about Bible reading?

4. Mortimer J. Adler and Charles Van Doren, *How to Read a Book*, rev. ed. (New York: Simon and Schuster, 1972), p. 49.

BORN
TO BE BATTERED

. . . the lovin' phone call book.

—UNDERLINE IT
—CIRCLE THINGS
—WRITE IN THE MARGINS
—TURN DOWN PAGE CORNERS

The more you use it,
        the more valuable it gets to be.

Reprinted by permission of South Central Bell Telephone.

D. TABLE OR DESK

It goes without saying that if you do more recording than just a few marks on the page of your Bible, you
need to use a table or desk. This leaves ample space for
paper, notebook, and other Bible versions. For analytical
Bible reading, it is practically a necessity that you work
at a table or desk.

II. Personal Preparation

It sounds so obvious and simplistic that it is easy to
overlook one of the keys to effective Bible reading. That
is *you*, the reader. Genuine Bible reading is never auto-

matic—it originates out of a heart that hungers to know what God has said. Geoffrey Thomas writes:

> The Christian life is paved with the best intentions of reading the Scriptures regularly, and also with many broken resolutions and disappointments. Jesus exhorts us to search the Scriptures (John 5:39); that is, we are to ransack the Word of God, to pore over it, to subject it to every kind of analysis, to grasp its every shade of meaning. We are to be obsessed with a desire to understand it. This passionate concern is never to become incidental or secondary. It should be a priority in the Christian life, an activity around which our existence revolves. If man cannot live by bread alone but by every word which proceeds out of the mouth of God, then God's Word must have an absolutely basic place in the whole of our Christian life. To its reading we must apply ourselves with the utmost industry.[5]

Do you love God, the Author of the Book? Do you have the joy of the psalmist who said, "My heart and my flesh sing for joy to the living God" (Psalm 84:2)? Do you crave to know more about Jesus, the key person of the Book? Do you give the Holy Spirit His rightful place in your heart (Romans 8:9) as your Teacher and Guide (John 16:13)? Beware of a barren intellectualism that reads the Bible through tinted glasses of vanity, as though you can understand it all, by yourself.

A. ATTITUDES FOR GOOD READING

Bible reading can be barren and even inaccurate, if we have the wrong attitudes. Let's look at some of the good attitudes that should cradle our Bible reading.

1. *Reverence.* The Bible is God's written Word to us. How important for us to revere its pages of truth, as it

5. Geoffrey Thomas, *Reading the Bible* (Carlisle, Pa.: Banner of Truth, 1980), p. 6.

tells about the God we worship. Someone has said, "Access to the inmost sanctuary of the Holy Scriptures is granted only to those who come to worship." Of course we do not worship the Book, but the God of the Book.

A deep conviction of the authority and infallibility of the Scriptures is of paramount importance for the one who reads its pages. The very words (verbal) and all the words (plenary), of the original writings must be recognized, in faith, as infallible and inerrant. The Bible should be seen as a *miracle book* as to its birth, its growth into one canon, its transmission (copyings and printings) through the centuries, its translations, and its world-wide reception. Bible reading keeps its glow when we revere it as God's miracle book.

2. *Desire*. It is one thing to *know* that we need to read the Bible. It is another thing to *desire* to read it. Such a desire is not forced, but should come naturally to the one who knows the Author personally and loves His fellowship. This is what Peter had in mind when he wrote, "long for the pure milk of the word . . . if you have tasted the kindness of the Lord" (1 Peter 2:2-3).

3. *Receptivity*. This is the attitude of submission and moldability. We approach the Bible not to do something to it, but to let it do something to us. With an open heart and mind, we are prepared to understand the Scriptures (Luke 24:45).

4. *Humility*. Humility is a virtue that God values in every aspect of our lives, because He wants us always to acknowledge who we really are and who He truly is. Don't aspire to be a *great* and *wonderful* student of the Word. Recognize your own limitations and the Spirit's role as Teacher, and always have as your goal in Bible reading and study to "grow in the grace and knowledge of our Lord and Savior Jesus Christ" (2 Peter 3:18).

When you feel discouraged over difficult passages of Scripture, recall that even Peter realized there were parts of Paul's epistles that were hard to understand (2 Peter 3:16).

B. FRESH APPROACH

Physically speaking, the best hours for reading are when the mind and body are most alert and relaxed, not weary from the tasks and responsibilities of the day.

From a spiritual standpoint, it is obvious that when you read the Bible you won't arrive at a keen perception of the text if there is spiritual dearth and confusion in your heart, which is often traced to unforgiven sins and a forsaking of your first love of Christ (Revelation 2:4). If you are enthusiastic and deeply grateful for your salvation and daily walk with Christ, it will show in your Bible reading. Here is how someone has put it:

> My experience is that the Bible is dull when I am dull. When I am really alive and set upon the text with a tidal pressure of living affinities, it opens, it multiplies discoveries, and reveals depths even faster than I can note them.[6]

Your approach to the Bible should be as keen and expectant as that of the explorer who gazes for the first time into a hitherto undiscovered cave. Doesn't it excite you to know that the Bible always contains a mine of eternal gems, waiting to be found and owned?

From a mental and psychological standpoint, approach a passage you are about to read *as though you had never seen it before.* Without this check, the oft-read and memorized phrase or verse may all too easily look trite or unimpressive. How often has the rhythmically read

6. Horace Bushnell, quoted in Robert Traina, *Methodical Bible Study* (n.p.: Robert Traina, 1952), p. 13.

"verily, verily" ("truly, truly") lost its impact because of its familiar sound?

C. TIME AND TOIL

Where do we *find* time to read the Bible? The answer is, Time will never be *found*. So we must *take* time to read the Bible, scheduling it at a regular time, if possible, each day. Someone has said, "We ought to have a Medo-Persian hour—an unchangeable hour for our Bible study." This is not an impossible nor unreasonable demand, seeing how easily we can schedule the daily reading of the newspaper and the weekly reading of periodicals. There is no substitute for being alone with God and His Word.

Don't wait for an opportune time to begin reading your Bible. Begin *now*. It is very true for Bible reading that the biggest waste of time is the time wasted in getting started.

And we must grant that Bible reading is toil. That is because when we read the Bible we are *doing* something, concentrating our whole being on a very important *task*, albeit exciting and fruitful. Some passages may be tedious or long; other passages may be obscure or difficult. And we wonder if we can ever reach the point of exhausting the Bible—but it can never be exhausted!

So Bible reading is work, but it is blessed work, and fruitful. If you believe this, it will make you a better reader.

III. Preliminary Checks

Bible reading isn't a spontaneous exercise, begun on the spur of a moment, out of nowhere. There are some things you should do before the reading, to set the stage. We'll call this *preliminary checks*. They apply to all three kinds of reading: devotional, analytical, and informational. Once you have chosen which kind of reading you will do, you are ready to make the preliminary checks described below. Whenever possible, record on paper the observations you make in these preliminary checks.

A. CHOOSE A BOOK OF THE SIXTY-SIX BOOK [7]

First decide if the reading will be in the Old Testament or in the New. Then choose which book of that Testament you want to read. In long-range planning of a Bible reading schedule, it is good to alternate between the New and Old Testaments. For example, read first a gospel (NT); then Genesis (OT); then Acts or an epistle (NT): then Exodus (OT), and so forth. Your choice of a book is usually determined by what it is that you want to learn, in what setting.

B. IDENTIFY THE TYPE OF WRITING TYPE

When we recognize the *type* of writing in a Bible passage, we are helping ourselves to listen more accurately to what God is saying and especially *how* He is saying it. Let us never forget that the Bible writers used a variety of ways to communicate the eternal truths. Why shouldn't we read and respond accordingly?

1. *Prose or poetry.* A Bible passage is either prose or poetry. Prose is the common, ordinary way of expressing something, like the narrative of Paul's voyage to Rome (Acts 27:1—28:31); Matthew's reporting of Jesus' crucifixion on the cross (Matthew 27:33-50); or Paul's counsel to Timothy (2 Timothy 4:1-8). Poetry is verse that is usually written line-by-line, condensed, beautiful, intensive expression of thought, like Psalm 23. Much of the Old Testament is poetry—even outside the poetic books of Job, Psalms, Proverbs, Ecclesiastes, and Song of Solo-

---

7. We will use the boxed indicators to aid us later to identify where we are at any point of study in our examples.

mon. For example, scan the prophetic books of Isaiah and Jeremiah in the NIV or NASB, and you will see from the format that much of those books is poetic. The main feature of Hebrew poetry is a rhythm of thought (rather than of sound). The poem is usually a succession of couplets, which are two lines related to each other in some way (Psalm 51:2). Sometimes there are three lines (Isaiah 41:5) or even four (Psalm 27:1). Observe these characteristics of poetry in the NASB text of Psalm 103:1-14 (fig. 2.4).

Psalm 103:1-14

Praise for the LORD's Mercies.

A Psalm of David.

[a] Bless the LORD, O my soul;
And all that is within me, *bless* His [b]holy name.
2   Bless the LORD, O my soul,
And [a]forget none of His benefits;
3   Who [a]pardons all your iniquities;
Who [b]heals all your diseases;
4   Who [a]redeems your life from the pit;
Who [b]crowns you with lovingkindness and compassion;
5   Who [a]satisfies your [1]years with good things,
So that your youth is [b]renewed like the eagle.

6   The LORD [a]performs [1]righteous deeds,
And judgments for all who are [b]oppressed.
7   He [a]made known His ways to Moses,
His [b]acts to the sons of Israel.
8   The LORD is [a]compassionate and gracious,
[b]Slow to anger and abounding in lovingkindness.
9   He [a]will not always strive *with us*;
Nor will He [b]keep *His anger* forever.
10   He has [a]not dealt with us according to our sins,
Nor rewarded us according to our iniquities.
11   For high [a]as the heavens are above the earth,
So great is His lovingkindness toward those who [1]fear Him.
12   As far as the east is from the west,
So far has He [a]removed our transgressions from us.
13   Just [a]as a father has compassion on *his* children,
So the LORD has compassion on those who [1]fear Him.
14   For [a]He Himself knows [1]our frame;
He [b]is mindful that we are *but* [c]dust.

Fig. 2.4

If your passage is poetry, be prepared to read it line by line. If it is prose, you may expect sentences of many words (e.g., in the New Testament epistles).

Figures of speech are prominent in poems, and we will look at those separately.

2. *Description or action.* A Bible passage is either mainly description, mainly action, or a moderate blending of each of those.

3. *Different objectives.* Most of the Bible instructs by historical narrative, but the remainder reveals a variety of objectives: teaching (doctrine), prophecy, testimony, appeal, prayer, and worship.

4. *Literal or figurative.* All Bible words are intended to be read either literally or figuratively. Figurative words are picture words that represent or describe something. Literal words tell the truths and facts directly. In the phrase "Jehovah my fortress," *Jehovah* is literal—it is the real name of a real Person. *Fortress* is figurative, intended to describe attributes of Jehovah. Jehovah is not a literal stone fortress.

Most of the Bible uses literal rather than figurative language. Some books, such as Revelation, use much figurative speech. In preliminary checks you should determine the book's overall type of writing, whether literal or figurative.

Bible authors use different kinds of figures of speech to communicate their message. If your passage is poetry, you can expect to see many of these. The descriptions given below are included here to help you identify a passage as poetic. (It is important that you read the Bible examples given with each figure.)

a) Metaphor—an implied comparison (not actually stated) between two unlike things (Isaiah 1:31)

b) Simile—an expressed comparison, using the word "like" (Psalm 59:6) *c)* Synecdoche—a part is used for the whole, or the whole for a part (Jeremiah 25:29)

d) Apostrophe—the writer addresses a thing or person that is absent or imaginary (Psalm 68:16)

e) Personification—attributing personal characteristics to things that do not have them (Psalm 77:16)

f) Hyperbole—deliberate exaggeration for emphasis (Psalm 119:136)

g) Irony—saying the opposite of what is meant, to emphasize something (Job 12:2)

Figures of speech add beauty, vividness, and emphasis to language. T. Norton Sterrett tells why it is valuable to recognize them:

> If we can recognize and interpret them in the Bible, God's Word will come to us with greater strength and clarity. In fact recognizing them may help us to understand verses that otherwise may appear to be contradictory. God's Word is rich with meaning. Thank him for these figures that add to our comprehension of that meaning.[8]

Your main objective in identifying the *type* of passage in this stage of preliminary checks is to adjust the focus of your "reading glasses" to the way the biblical author wrote the passage.

C. RELATE THE BOOK TO ITS GENERAL SETTING $\boxed{\text{SETTING}}$

Think for a few minutes about where the book is in relation to its original setting. (See the chart, Bible

8. T. Norton Sterrett, *How to Understand Your Bible* (Downers Grove, Ill.: InterVarsity, 1974), p. 101.

Content and World History, fig. 1.5. Also, refer to the
Old Testament History chart, Appendix 5.) A look at a
survey book of the Testament that is involved will give
you further help in knowing the general setting of the
book.[9]

D. DECIDE ON THE PASSAGE TO BE READ | PASSAGE |

Now you must determine what passage you will be
reading, if it is not the whole book. Two things are
involved in your choice: unit and length.

1. *Unit.* Whatever the length of the passage you
read, it should be a full unit. Here are the possible
choices:

- *a)* Verse. Most of the verses of the Bible are the
  length of one sentence. There are exceptions to
  this. For example, read Hebrews 1:1-2 (NASB)
  and observe that verse 1 is incomplete without
  verse 2. So the *unit* is not one verse, but two.[10]

- *b)* Paragraph. A paragraph is a unit. It is a group of
  verses communicating one main thought. Most
  Bible editions show paragraph divisions in some
  way—the more prominent, the better. If you
  feel that your Bible edition does not show a
  good series of paragraph divisions for a segment
  that you are reading, consult other versions, beginning with the *New Berkeley Version* or *New
  International Version.*

- *c)* Segment. A segment is also a unit. It is a group
  of paragraphs, getting across one main topic.

9. See Irving L. Jensen, *Jensen's Survey of the New Testament* (Chicago: Moody, 1981) and *Jensen's Survey of the Old Testament* (Chicago: Moody, 1978).
10. Read Judges 20:27-28 for an example of poor verse division—in
   the middle of a parenthesis!

Sometimes it is the length of one chapter. It is a very practical length for Bible reading and study. Example: the long chapter of John 1 (51 verses) is made up of three segments: 1:1-18; 1:19-39; 1:40-51.[11] Most of your Bible reading will be of the length of a segment. It is the length recommended for analytical reading and study.

d) Section. A section is a group of segments, or a large part of a book. For example, Acts has three sections:

1:1—8:1a	Church Established
8:1b—12:25	Church Scattered
13:1—28:31	Church Extended

2. *Length.* The length of the passage you read will vary from time to time. The following three things should play an important part in the length you decide on:

a) Fulfillment of your objectives. Does the passage say enough about the subject, or should you include more verses (before or after)?

b) Substance. Does the passage have enough substance for the subject? For example, after twenty verses that list family names, you may want to include the paragraph that follows if it offers counsel from God.

c) Practicality. Bible reading and study should always be practical, especially as to time involved in your activities.

11. The NIV shows good segment headings in connection with the Bible text. The inductive study guides by this author, *Bible Self-Study Guides* (Moody Press) and *Do-It-Yourself Bible Studies* (Here's Life Publishers), go through the Bible segment by segment.

Hebrews 12:2-17 (NASB)

Ryrie Study Bible

nesses surrounding us, let ᵃus also ᵇlay aside every encumbrance, and the sin which so easily entangles us, and let us ᶜrun with ᵈendurance the race that is set before us,

2:10 ᵇPhil. 2:8f., Heb. 2:9 ᶜ1 Cor. 1:18, 23; Heb. 13:13 ᵈHeb. 1:3

2 fixing our eyes on Jesus, the ᵃauthor and perfecter of faith, who for the joy set before Him ᵇendured the cross, ᶜdespising the shame, and has ᵈsat down at the right hand of the throne of God.

2 *The disciplines of life,*
    12:3-11

★ 3 ᵃMatt. 10:24; Rev. 2:3 ᵇGal. 6:9; Heb. 12:5

3 For ᵃconsider Him who has endured such hostility by sinners against Himself, so that you may not grow weary ᵇand lose heart.

★ 4 ᵃHeb. 10:32ff. 13:13 ᵇPhil. 2:8

4 ᵃYou have not yet resisted ᵇto the point of shedding blood in your striving against sin;

★ 5-11 5 ᵃProv. 3:11 ᵇHeb. 12:3

5 and you have forgotten the exhortation which is addressed to you as sons,

    "ᵃMY SON, DO NOT REGARD
        LIGHTLY THE DISCIPLINE OF
        THE LORD,
    NOR ᵇFAINT WHEN YOU ARE
        REPROVED BY HIM;

6 ᵃProv. 3:12 ᵇPs. 119:75; Rev. 3:19

6 ᵃFOR THOSE ᵇWHOM THE
        LORD LOVES HE DISCI-
        PLINES,
    AND HE SCOURGES EVERY SON
        WHOM HE RECEIVES."

7 ᵃDeut. 8:5; 2 Sam. 7:14; Prov. 13:24; 19:18; 23:13f.

7 It is for discipline that you endure; ᵃGod deals with you as with sons; for what son is there whom *his* father does not discipline?

8 ᵃ1 Pet. 5:9

8 But if you are without discipline, ᵃof which all have become

partakers, then you are illegitimate children and not sons.

9 ᵃLuke 18:2 ᵇNum. 16:22; 27:16; Rev. 22:6 ᶜIs. 38:16

9 Furthermore, we had earthly fathers to discipline us, and we ᵃrespected them; shall we not much rather be subject to ᵇthe Father of spirits, and ᶜlive?

10 ᵃ2 Pet. 1:4

10 For they disciplined us for a short time as seemed best to them, but He disciplines us for *our* good, ᵃthat we may share His holiness.

11 ᵃ1 Pet. 1:6 ᵇIs. 32:17; 2 Tim. 4:8; James 3:17f.

11 All discipline ᵃfor the moment seems not to be joyful, but sorrowful; yet to those who have been trained by it, afterwards it yields the ᵇpeaceful fruit of righteousness.

3 *The direction of life,*
    12:12-17

12 ᵃIs. 35:3

12 Therefore, ᵃstrengthen the hands that are weak and the knees that are feeble,

13 ᵃProv. 4:26; Gal. 2:14 ᵇGal. 6:1; James 5:16 14 ᵃRom. 14:19 ᵇRom. 6:22; Heb. 12:10 ᶜMatt. 5:8; Heb. 9:28

13 and ᵃmake straight paths for your feet, so that *the limb* which is lame may not be put out of joint, but rather ᵇbe healed.
14 ᵃPursue peace with all men, and the ᵇsanctification without which no one will ᶜsee the Lord.

15 ᵃ2 Cor. 6:1; Gal. 5:4; Heb. 4:1 ᵇDeut. 29:18 ᶜTitus 1:15

15 See to it that no one ᵃcomes short of the grace of God; that no ᵇroot of bitterness springing up causes trouble, and by it many be ᶜdefiled;

★16 ᵃHeb. 13:4 ᵇ1 Tim. 1:9 ᶜGen. 25:33f.

16 that *there* be no ᵃimmoral or ᵇgodless person like Esau, ᶜwho sold his own birthright for a *single* meal.

17 ᵃGen. 27:30-40

17 For you know that even afterwards, ᵃwhen he desired to inherit the blessing, he was rejected, for he found no place for

---

faith mentioned in chapter 11 and others. *every encumbrance.* That which hinders the believer from being a winner. *the sin which so easily entangles us.* I.e., unbelief.
12:3 *Him.* Jesus.
12:4 *You have not yet resisted to the point of shedding blood.* None of the readers of this book had yet been martyred.
12:5-11 In these verses the writer discusses why Christians are disciplined. (1) It is part of the educational process by which a believer is fitted to share God's holiness (v. 10). (2) It is

proof of a genuine love relationship between the heavenly Father and His children (vv. 6, 8). (3) It helps train them to be obedient (v. 9). (4) It produces the fruit of righteousness in their lives (v. 11). For additional teaching on this subject see the book of Job; Rom. 8:18; 2 Cor. 1:3-4; 4:16-17; 12:7-9; Phil. 1:29; 2 Tim. 3:12.
12:16 *Esau.* See Gen. 25:33. Though he may not have been *immoral* in the physical sense, Esau was immoral in the spiritual sense, being worldly and materialistic.

Fig. 2.5

The standard length of reading is that of a segment, or an average chapter. For devotions, especially in the deeper doctrinal portions of the Bible, you may find it advantageous to meditate on no more than a paragraph or even a verse. In determining the length of the passage to be read, remember that you want to read that which can be read *thoroughly*.

For a long-range project of devotional reading, some have chosen to read through the Bible in a year, which involves three to four chapters a day (there are 1189 chapters in the Bible). A more practical plan is to read through the Bible in three years (about one chapter a day). See a suggested three-year schedule in Appendix 6. The important thing is not how many times you've gone through the Bible, but whether the Bible has gone through you.

E. CHECK ON MARGINAL NOTES AND OLD TESTAMENT QUOTES

1. *Marginal notes.* MN Many Bible editions include notes that appear either in the margins, or in a center column, or at the bottom of the page. The notes include cross-reference Bible verses, alternate text readings, or commentary. See the page from the *Ryrie Study Bible* (fig. 2.5) on Hebrews 12:2-17.

The alternate text readings will have a bearing on your reading of the passage. Jot down the latter under MN on paper, or mark your Bible text in some manner to show the readings.

2. *Quotes from the Old Testament.* QU Make the quick but important observation of any quotes the passage includes from the Old Testament. See Hebrews 12:5-6 in figure 2.5.

F. SCAN THE SURROUNDING PASSAGES

The immediate setting of a passage can be one of the best aids to learning its meaning. For example, a

IV. Preliminary Checks for Reading a Passage

Matthew 3:1-17 (NIV)

3 In those days John the Baptist came, preaching in the desert of Judea [2]and saying, "Repent, for the kingdom of heaven is near." [3]This is he who was spoken of through the prophet Isaiah:

"A voice of one calling in the desert,
'Prepare the way for the Lord,
    make straight paths for him.' " [b]

[4]John's clothes were made of camel's hair, and he had a leather belt around his waist. His food was locusts and wild honey. [5]People went out to him from Jerusalem and all Judea and the whole region of the Jordan. [6]Confessing their sins, they were baptized by him in the Jordan River.

[7]But when he saw many of the Pharisees and Sadducees coming to where he was baptizing, he said to them: "You brood of vipers! Who warned you to flee from the coming wrath? [8]Produce fruit in keeping with repentance. [9]And do not think you can say to yourselves, 'We have Abraham as our father.' I tell you that out of these stones God can raise up children for Abraham. [10]The ax is already at the root of the trees, and every tree that does not produce good fruit will be cut down and thrown into the fire.

[11]"I baptize you with[a] water for repentance. But after me will come one who is more powerful than I, whose sandals I am not fit to carry. He will baptize you with the Holy Spirit and with fire. [12]His winnowing fork is in his hand, and he will clear his threshing floor, gathering the wheat into his barn and burning up the chaff with unquenchable fire."

[13]Then Jesus came from Galilee to the Jordan to be baptized by John. [14]But John tried to deter him, saying, "I need to be baptized by you, and do you come to me?"

[15]Jesus replied, "Let it be so now; it is proper for us to do this to fulfill all righteousness." Then John consented.

[16]As soon as Jesus was baptized, he went up out of the water. At that moment heaven was opened, and he saw the Spirit of God descending on him like a dove. [17]And a voice from heaven said, "This is my Son, whom I love; with him I am well-pleased."

[b]3 Isaiah 40:3   [a]11 Or in

Fig. 2.6

good clue to the main point of a parable is what brought it on, as revealed in the paragraph preceding it.

1. *What goes before?* ┃ BEF ┃ The verse or paragraph just before the beginning of your passage is usually a good indicator of preceding context.

2. *What follows after?* ┃ AFT ┃ Two examples of such clues are reactions to a speech and explanation of a doctrine just recorded.

3. *What is the continuity?* ┃ CON ┃ For any one passage, you should be able to identify the continuity of the three parts: before, here, and after.

Let's now go through the preliminary checks for Matthew 3:1-17.

┃ BOOK ┃ The book I have chosen is the gospel according to Matthew.

┃ TYPE ┃ Matthew is not poetry; it is prose. It is historical narrative, mainly action, recording literally things that happened and words that were spoken.

┃ SETTING ┃ Matthew is the first of the New Testament books that record the life of Jesus. It is a good connecting link between the Old Testament and the New Testament books that follow it. It reveals truths about Jesus' kingdom now and to come.

┃ PASSAGE ┃ The unit I have selected is the segment 3:1-17. In our Bibles this is also shown as one full chapter. The NIV text shows this segment to be divided into six paragraphs. (Verses 13-15 are really just one paragraphical unit—the NIV shows two paragraphs because conversation is involved.) I have underscored these paragraph divisions in my Bible by drawing pencil lines at the opening verses. This marking of paragraph divisions is one of the best and simplest "habits" in the reading process that I can take on.

The length of this passage is good for my present reading project. A glance at the text shows that it has solid content.

MN The marginal notes (footnotes) of NIV are scanty, so I may want to compare the notes of another version, like NASB. For the phrase "baptize you with water" (v. 11), NIV gives an alternate translation, "baptize you in water."

QU Matthew quotes the prophet Isaiah in verse 3. The footnote shows the source as Isaiah 40:3. I read this in its original setting in the Old Testament, and compare the two settings.

BEF I read the preceding paragraph, 2:19-23. It is about the infant Jesus and His parents settling down in the town of Nazareth.

AFT The first words (4:1) following the Father's commendation of His Son (3:17) narrate the Spirit's leading Jesus into a deserted place to be tempted by the devil.

CON I see a continuity in Matthew's report:

Chapters 1-2—Jesus' coming to the world, at His
                birth
Chapter 3—Jesus' coming to a public ministry
Chapter 4—first test of that ministry

The preliminary checks described in these pages apply to all three kinds of reading we will be looking at in the remainder of this book. We will look at devotional reading first because it is the most common.

3

The Activities of Devotional Reading △

Devotional reading is mainly a reflective time of reading the Bible alone with God. It is not a legalistic, pietistic exercise to fulfill an obligation, but an act of worship for the child of God who seeks to become more familiar with God and with His Word. Charles Swindoll gives four reasons he values private devotions:

1) It keeps his heart warm.
2) It allows time for the Lord to speak to him.
3) It gives him insight into life itself.
4) It makes him come to terms with things that mar his fellowship with the Lord.[1]

Let's never forget what a wonderful, happy privilege it is to meet with our Lord and listen to Him speak.

I. Requirements for Effective Reading

Common to all kinds of Bible reading is the reading itself. So this is a good time and place to discuss

1. Charles Swindoll, "Devotional Bible Study," *Christianity Today,* 8 October 1982, p. 54.

what makes our reading effective, whether in devotions, analysis, or information-seeking. The ultimate purposes of all Bible reading pursue this route for their fulfillment:

OBSERVATION—What does the text say?
INTERPRETATION—What does that mean?
APPLICATION—How should I apply this?

Notice that observation comes first. This is the reading stage. Let's see what makes the reading effective.

A. READ CAREFULLY

The underlying conviction of this appeal is that every part of Scripture is divinely inspired and is vital. God has spoken. Read alertly, not mechanically. There is a place at other times for the quick-yet-careful, cursive reading, but in devotional analytical reading you must read deliberately and slowly, weighing each word—even the punctuation. Each word in the Bible has a function. Always seek to learn what that is.

B. READ REPEATEDLY

Good readers read a passage many times. Return often to the beginning of the passage. One thrust of the spade does not unearth all the gems of the Bible's mine. Don't ever conclude that you have exhausted the meaning of a verse when it becomes familiar to you. John Bunyan said that old truths are always new to us if they come with the aroma of heaven upon them. One of the valuable by-products of repeated readings is the memorization of the Bible text.

C. READ ALOUD

It is amazing how some words and phrases will take on a sharper and brighter look when they are read aloud. Try reading the passage aloud at least once, as slowly as you feel is necessary.

D. READ AT DIFFERENT SPEEDS

There are really only three speeds of reading: fast, slow, and moderate. Fast reading has the benefit of emphasizing highlights and general movements of the text. A moderate pace is the speed of most reading, and this has its natural advantages. Bible readers have not spent enough of their time at the slow pace and are the losers for it. It is possible to tour a country so fast that one does not really see the land. Such a person has been called a "tripper," in contrast to the traveler, who journeys slowly to absorb not only the sights, but also the sounds and the aromas. The Rustic Roads System of Wisconsin came into being because of the vision of Earl Skagen, a highway commissioner, who saw the pretty back roads of the state giving way to super highways. "I've been advocating good highways all my life, but I think there should be two kinds of roads—roads where people can drive slowly, bike or walk, leisurely enjoying the countryside, and excellent highways that move people in a hurry."[2]

Study the Bible as a traveler who is not pushed by any impulse to dart off to the next stop. Gaze long across its fields of truths. Climb its mountains of vision. Cross its valleys of trial. Cool yourself in its streams of inspiration. Take in all you can as the Holy Spirit guides you through its many halls of instruction.

Even as you think of the above illustrations of moving about in your Bible reading, it may strike you that rereading is a natural outcome of slow reading, in fact, rereading *is* slow reading. James Sire, in writing on how to read slowly, says:

2. Diane K. Gentry, "Wisconsin's Rustic Roads," *Modern Maturity*, June-July 1984, p. 64.

Reading speed is totally irrelevant. In fact, over and over in the next few chapters I will ask you to read and then re-read. . . . Good readers re-read many things many times.[3]

E. READ RECREATIVELY

In recreative reading you put yourself in the passage you are reading. If it is ancient Old Testament history, try to visualize the action as happening now, with you in it. "Precisely because God chose to speak in the context of real human history, we may take courage that these same words will speak again and again in our own 'real' history, as they have throughout the history of the church."[4] If geographical places are involved, picture a map showing areas, roads, and rivers. If the text reads that Jesus "had to pass through Samaria" (John 4:4), visualize the geography first, as you look for an answer to your question, "Why?" Get yourself involved with the *feelings* of the passage you are reading. To visualize is to empathize.

F. READ WITH TOOLS IN HAND

When you read your Bible, always have a marking pencil (or pen) in hand, and paper (or notebook) on a table or desk next to your Bible. This is the best setup for a Bible reading experience.

The valuable help of your pencil cannot be overstated. Professor Louis Agassiz of Harvard was once approached by a student concerning the study of a special area of zoology. Agassiz gave him a pickled specimen of a fish, a haemulon, which was to be the sole object of his scrutiny for days to come.

Dr. Agassiz's advice to the student was very practi-

3. James W. Sire, *How to Read Slowly* (Downers Grove, Ill.: Inter-Varsity, 1978), p. 21.
4. Gordon D. Fee and Douglas Stuart, *How to Read the Bible for All Its Worth* (Grand Rapids: Zondervan, 1982), p. 20.

cal and to the point: (1) He was to "look, look, look," for how else could he master the subject? (2) He was to draw on paper what he saw, for "the pencil is one of the best eyes." (3) He was to see the parts of the fish in their orderly arrangement and in relation to one another because, in the professor's blunt words, "facts are stupid things until brought into connection with some general law."

For three whole days the student kept following the advice of his teacher, and in doing so he learned just about all there was to know about the haemulon. In fact, so absorbed was he in the learning process and so indelible was the impression of the haemulon that years later he testified, "To this day, if I attempt to draw a fish, I can draw nothing but haemulons."

I am convinced that a *pencil in hand* is the best mechanical aid that you can use in a reading project.

G. READ TO UNDERSTAND

Your observations of the Bible text should make you want to understand what it means. One writer puts it this way: "If you are *really* reading, therefore, when you pick up a page of print, something happens. You react to that page immediately. A chain reaction begins."[5] You begin to ask questions like,

> What is the main point of this passage?
> How is the writer getting it across?
> What truths and facts is he emphasizing?
> How does he relate truths to each other?
> What is my purpose in reading this?

God wants us to understand His Book. Read the story of a very important day in the life of the Israelites who returned to their homeland after captivity in Bab-

5. Paul D. Leedy, *Improve Your Reading* (New York: McGraw-Hill, 1956), p. 14.

ylon. The passage is Nehemiah 8:1-8. The leaders read
to the people "from the book, from the law of God,
translating to give the sense" so that the people "understood the reading" (8:8).

H. REFLECT AS YOU READ

When God speaks to us, we should stand still and
consider what He is saying. In Bible reading, reflection is
the mind and heart at work, thinking over what the
eyes have seen. That is quite different from merely seeing with the eye, which is what someone has labeled
"retinizing." Reflection in Bible reading should have the
intensity of meditation, whereby the soul has the desire
and intention of obeying God's Word. "You shall meditate on it day and night, so that you may be careful to *do*
according to all that is written in it" (Joshua 1:8, italics
added).

How should we reflect on the Scriptures? Here are
some suggestions.

1. *Reflect purposefully.* Purpose is natural. "You don't
just read. You read for a reason, a purpose, with a particular aim in mind."[6] The psalmist had a purpose in
hiding God's Word in his heart: that he might not sin
against God (Psalm 119:11). The Berean Christians had a
purpose in examining the Scriptures daily: that they
might know the truth (Acts 17:11).

Bible meditation should not be haphazard, or piece-
meal. If you want to keep a fire burning in your soul,
don't scatter its fuel. Also, recall the "seed-pickers" of
Paul's day who flitted here and there, picking up bits of
talk about any subject, arriving at no good conclusions.
(Paul was falsely accused of being a seed-picker in Acts
17:18, where the word is translated "babbler" in the
NIV.) Reading only isolated verses, out of context, and

6. Ibid., p. 159.

expanding them according to personal whims, is a dangerous practice. It is as foolish and fruitless to read the Bible without purpose as it is to search about a room looking for nothing in particular.

What are your purposes as you meditate on the Scriptures? Do you want to know God more intimately, and glorify Him? Do you want to know more about yourself? Do you want to grow strong spiritually? Do you want to know God's will, hear a word of comfort, receive a challenge? Then reflect purposefully!

2. *Reflect imaginatively.* This is not difficult, if you are willing to put yourself into the situation of the Bible passage. Taste and feel every word you read. The great translator Miles Coverdale wrote to a friend once, "Now I begyne to taste of Holy Schryptures; now (honour be to God) I am sett to the most swete smell of holy lettyres."

If the passage is narrative, visualize the setting. Take this verse as an example: "He ordered the crowd to sit down on the ground. Then he took the seven loaves, gave thanks to God, broke them, and gave them to his disciples to distribute to the crowd; and the disciples did so" (Mark 8:6, TEV*). Try meditating on this verse imagining yourself as one of the crowd, or as one of the disciples. Such exercise can give birth to many keen insights.

If the passage is doctrine or exhortation, put yourself in the middle of it, for after all, are you not the pupil being taught? Try this with Colossians 2:3 (TEV): "He [Christ] is the key that opens all the hidden treasures of God's wisdom and knowledge." Imagine how rich you are in Christ!

Reflect imaginatively also on passages that do not pertain to you now as a Christian. Do you shudder when you meditate on verses like Luke 13:27-28: "I do

Today's English Version (Good News for Modern Man).

not know where you are from . . . depart from me . . . there will be weeping and gnashing of teeth"? Do such verses cause you to exclaim "There am I but for the grace of God"? Do they challenge you concerning the hundreds of thousands of souls passing away daily into a Christless eternity? Years ago a seminary graduating class heard these words from the speaker: "Would that upon the naked, palpitating heart of each one of you might be laid one red hot coal of God Almighty's wrath!"

Something is bound to stir within your soul the moment you begin to reflect imaginatively as you read the Bible.

3. *Reflect humbly.* The Word you are reading is the *holy* Word of the *holy* God. God is bigger than His Book. As someone has said, "Behind and beneath the Bible, above and beyond the Bible, is the God of the Bible." It should humble you to think that this Holy One, who is also the Almighty One, has spoken to you in the Bible and has given you the blessed privilege to read it, and so to listen to Him.

When you open your Bible to read it and reflect on it, remember that this is *The Holy Bible*, a title given to no other book in the world. The translators of the King James Version recognized this, as borne out by these words contained in their introduction:

"The original thereof from heaven, not from earth;
   the inditer: the Holy Spirit, not the wit of the
          apostles or prophets;
   the penmen: those that were sanctified from the
          womb and endowed with a principal
          portion of God's Spirit;
   the matter: verity, purity, uprightness;
   the form: God's Word, God's testimony, God's ora-
          cles, the Word of Truth, the Word of
          Salvation, the Light of Understanding;

the stableness of persuasion: repentance from dead
        works, newness of life, holiness,
        peace and joy in the Holy Ghost.
Happy is the man that delighteth in this Holy
Word, and thrice happy he that meditateth in it
day and night."

4. *Reflect prayerfully.* If you reflect humbly, you will
reflect prayerfully, for the contrite heart craves to speak
to the One on whom it depends. Bathe your reflection
in prayer, from beginning to end. Thank God for the
happy privilege of reading His Word. Ask Him to teach
you by His Holy Spirit, and to help you apply the Word
to your personal life. The greatest prayer ever prayed by
a man in connection with the Scriptures is the 119th
psalm. Study this psalm carefully to learn how to reflect
prayerfully on the Word. One example is cited here:
"Open my eyes, that I may behold wonderful things
from Thy law" (Psalm 119:18).

> Within that awful volume lies
> The mystery of mysteries!
> Happiest they of human race,
> To whom God has granted grace
> To read, to fear, to hope, to pray,
> To lift the latch, and force the way;
> And better that they'd ne'er been born,
> Who read to doubt, or read to scorn.
> (Sir Walter Scott, 1771-1832)

5. *Reflect patiently.* Patience in any phase of life is
priceless. The great naturalist Fabre always referred to
his two best instruments as "time" and "patience." Patience on the part of young Clyde Tombaugh is what led
him finally to discover the planet Pluto. After astrono-
mers calculated a probable orbit for this "suspected"
heavenly body, which they had never seen, Tombaugh

took up the search in March 1929. *Time* magazine records the investigation:

> He examined scores of telescopic photographs, each showing tens of thousands of star images, in pairs under the blink comparator, or dual microscope. It often took three days to scan a single pair. It was exhausting, eye-cracking work—in his own words, "brutal tediousness." And it went on for months. Star by star, he examined 20 million images. Then on February 18, 1930, as he was blinking at a pair of photographs in the constellation Gemini, "I suddenly came upon the image of Pluto!" It was the most dramatic astronomic discovery in nearly 100 years, and it was made possible by the patience of an American.[7]

The New Testament makes many references to the gem of Christian patience. Patience is surely a requirement in the meditative process of reading God's Word. In fact, the phrase "wait on the Lord" can be applied in meditation. Reflection requires time and concentration, and the good Bible student will give both. For his patience he will be rewarded with the pleasure and excitement of discovering stars of divine truth he has never seen before.

The call to reflection in Bible reading is expressed in Samuel's plain words to Saul, "Stand here thou still a while, that I may shew thee the word of God" (1 Samuel 9:27, KJV).

II. The Passage Is Paramount

There is something about devotional reading that especially magnifies and spotlights the Scripture passage itself. There is a minimum of activities, and you sense you are standing in a quiet spot of God's beautiful creation.

7. *Time*, 1 April 1966, p. 10.

But since there are ways and methods of devotional reading, there are some activities involved, especially mental and spiritual. And it is important to remember that rereadings are part of the devotional process. These are some of the things we will be looking at in the next pages.

A. PRELIMINARY CHECKS

Do you recall the preliminary checks discussed earlier? Let's apply these to devotional reading, in brief ways.

BOOK Some books are especially valuable for devotions. Included are books of worship (e.g., the Psalms); doctrine and practice (e.g., Philippians); and chosen narrative sections (e.g., the life of Christ).

TYPE If you choose a poetic book, you can expect to see many kinds of poetic ways of expressing the truths, such as metaphors and symbols. (Recall the discussion of this in chapter 2.)

SETTING The passage will mean much more to you if you can first identify its setting. For example, if you first know that Psalm 51 is David's contrite prayer for pardon after he had committed adultery with Bathsheba, then you will be more alert and compassionate as you read the psalm.

PASSAGE For devotions, the passage can be short or long, but it should be a unit (e.g., one paragraph). If the passage is a segment, determine where its paragraph divisions are.

MN It is wise to look at your Bible's marginal notes before you make even your first devotional reading. Record alternate readings in the margin.

$\boxed{\text{QU}}$ If there is an Old Testament quote in your passage, go back and identify its original setting.

$\boxed{\text{BEF}}$, $\boxed{\text{AFT}}$, and $\boxed{\text{CON}}$ Sometimes passages for devotional reading are erroneously taken out of context. You can avoid this by seeing what goes before your passage, what follows after, and what the continuity is.

B. SCANNING THE STRUCTURE

Let's say that you have chosen a segment of a Bible book as the passage for your devotional reading, and you have completed the preliminary checks. Now what? The answer is, Scan the structure of that segment. That is, see how the author put the words together in that one passage. This is not a thorough, analytical study—you may want to do that with the passage at a later time.

Here are things to look for in your brief survey of the structure of the passage. Note that rereadings of the text are involved.

1. Read the entire passage (segment) once, without being conscious of paragraph divisions. Do you detect a main purpose of the passage?

2. How many paragraphs does the segment have? Read each one separately. Does each one have a different subject or theme?

3. Observe the sentences of the segment. Are they long or short? Sometimes a long sentence is not clear, because its core (main subject, verb, object) is hidden among the many phrases. Pick out the core of such sentences, and mark your Bible accordingly.

4. Does the writer include commands or questions?

5. Each sentence is made up of phrases. A phrase is two or more words in sequence to form a unit. Skim the passage and observe the lengths of the phrases.

6. Words make up the phrases. Words are the "stuff," the visible divine substance of the Book. Words of the Bible communicate ideas from God to man. You

always want to be word-conscious in your Bible reading. Don't overlook small words in the midst of long words. Watch for feeling words—the Bible has much to say about our feelings. Look for attention-getting words, like *behold*.

7. Don't overlook punctuation, including the dash. These are the translators' way of holding together the phrases of a sentence in a clear, accurate way.

8. There are always some key words and phrases in a passage. These are words and phrases that stand out to you, in your various readings. Mark them in your Bible.

9. Look for lists of words, actions, or things in the passage.

10. Read the whole passage once again. Do you observe any turning point? How about a progression leading to a climax? Your passage may not have either of these, but you always want to look for them. They are some of the things that make Bible reading so exciting.

C. TONE

A Bible author can't avoid or overlook feeling and emotion in his writing, because the whole theme of Scripture—salvation by Jesus Christ—touches those feelings, directly or indirectly. It is a theme of life and death. So when you are reading a passage, especially in devotions, look for every feeling word or phrase. These can be important clues to the main purposes of the author in writing what he does.

D. RECASTING THE TEXT

Here is an exercise for you to do that can be one of the most enjoyable parts of your reading.[8] It is recasting or recreating the Bible text into what I call a *talking*

8. This is an optional part of devotional reading, but it can do much for you if you choose to complete it. It is an essential part of analytical reading, to be discussed later.

text—talking, because you make the printed page talk, especially the *emphasized* parts and the *related* parts. Here is what you do:

1. Read your passage again, making more marks in the printed text of your Bible, to show especially key words and phrases, and how parts are related to each other (underlinings, arrows, etc. can be used here).

2. Now recast the Bible text by printing it *phrase by phrase* on a piece of paper, letting the text "talk," to show emphases and relationships. For example, for emphasis, underline a word, or print it large. For relationship, draw a connecting arrow between two items, or number a list (1, 2, 3, etc.). The talking text of Romans 15:1-4 (fig. 3.1) shows ways to do this.[9]

Talking Text of Romans 15:1-4

1 Now we who are STRONG
        ought to bear the weaknesses
                                of those **without strength**
        and not just please ourselves.
2 Let each of us please his neighbor
            (1) for his GOOD,
            (2) to his EDIFICATION.
3 For even CHRIST did **not** please Himself;
        but as it is written,
        "The **reproaches** of those who **reproached**
        Thee **fell upon Me**."   [Ps. 69:9]
4 For whatever was written in earlier times
            was written FOR OUR INSTRUCTION,
        that
            (1) through PERSEVERANCE and
            (2) the ENCOURAGEMENT
                    of the SCRIPTURES
                        → we might have HOPE.

Fig. 3.1

9. Talking texts appear in each study unit of the *Do-It-Yourself Bible Studies* series by this author (Here's Life Publishers).

This talking text will help you much in the "devotional search" that follows, which is the main part of your devotional study.

III. Devotional Reading: A Spiritual Experience

Everything you have done up to this point is *preparation* for your devotional reading. This is *your* personal devotional time. It is part of your worship of God, when you talk to Him, and, more prominently, when He talks to you through His Word.

A. YOU ARE THE FOCAL POINT

Your devotional reading is part of your personal search for spiritual help, food, instruction, and inspiration. The question you keep asking is, How does this touch *me?* You identify with the persons of the Bible text, or with the original readers, or with the writer. *You* are the focal point. This is not a selfish outlook. It is why God gave the Book to you.

B. THE ARENA AND PERSPECTIVE OF YOUR SEARCH

The question, How does this touch me? is legitimate and natural to ask. The following pages will give answers and directions.

1. ARENA *observations.* Think of the Bible as a book about the *arena of life* in God's universe. The participants of that arena are shown in Figure 3.2.

These are the possible participants in any Bible passage:

- GOD (Father, Son, Spirit); His angels
- SATAN; his hosts
- PEOPLE of the world
- YOU, the reader of the passages

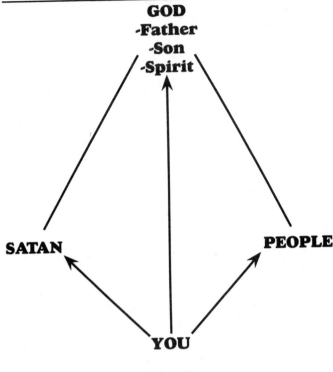

Fig. 3.2

The arena will be represented by this symbol: ◊

In your devotional reading it is your task to search the passage to observe what it says about the participants in the arena of life. These are your *arena* observations. It is important that you record these on paper. The kinds of observations you make will be illustrated in the example of a devotional reading of Romans 15:30-33 later in this chapter.

2. *Perspective.* You are reading the passage from *your* perspective. (This is the reason for the arrows moving from you to the other three points.) You may identify with a person in the passage, or, if people are not in the passage, you may ask this question, "What if *I* were there?"

C. RESPONSE AND APPLICATION

You leave the passage, for this time of devotional reading, only after you have made responses to it. All Bible study by a Christian, whether of a devotional or analytical nature, demands personal response. We are to practice what we read and reflect upon. This is the will in action. The Word was given to storm that will. It shouldn't surprise you how strongly the Bible calls for your response. God wants you to confess sin, believe Him, and obey His Word.

1. *Responding with confession.* Since the Bible is the Word of a holy God to people who sin, it is always searching out and exposing that sin. The Word cuts as a sword to the very inmost recesses of our being, where it "judges the desires and thoughts of men's hearts. There is nothing that can be hid from God" (Hebrews 4:12-13, TEV). Whenever you read the Bible, it should always be with a heart that acknowledges its sin, and confesses it to God. Then the channel is cleared for further communication with God, and the blessings of Bible reading begin to accrue.

2. *Responding in faith.* Faith involves every part of your Christian life, including your Bible reading. If you do not read the Bible believingly, you will lose out utterly. Hebrews 4:2 makes this very clear: "For indeed we have had good news preached to us, just as they also; but the word they heard did not profit them, because it was not united by faith in those who heard."

3. *Responding by obedience.* When we obey God's Word, we are demonstrating where our faith rests, and how strong it is. We may not always understand God's ways, but we must always walk in His steps.

Inescapably, you are related in some way to God, to Satan, and to other people, as well as to yourself. Here are listed some of the involvements of those relations. They are reminders to you of the kinds of applications that should come from your devotional reading.

Your Relationship to God
- fellowship to enjoy
- commands to obey
- promises to claim
- prayers to echo

Your Relationship to Satan
- person to resist
- devices to recognize
- sins to avoid and confess
- armor to wear

Your Relationship to Others
- in the home
- in the church
- in society
- in the world

Your Own Very Being
- past heritage
- present experience
- future hope

D. DIFFICULTIES IN THE PASSAGE

Some passages of Scripture are difficult to read and examine, no less to understand. In devotional reading, if the difficulty persists after repeated readings, it is best to set it aside for later analysis, and concentrate on the remainder of the passage. Don't let this interruption lessen the effectiveness of your devotions.

E. CONCLUDING MEDITATIONS AND PRAYER

The most relaxed minutes of your devotions should be the last ones, because God has been speaking to you in His Word, and you have been hearing and responding to it. Ask for His continued help, and thank Him for the portion of His Word that you have been reading.

The examples in the remainder of this chapter are given to demonstrate what is involved in the readings of actual passages. It should not surprise you that so much is involved in devotional reading. Recall from the earlier discussion that devotional reading *is reading*, and all reading, to be effective, is more than just a glance at the printed words.

IV. Devotional Reading of a Passage

Romans 15:30-33 (NASB)

30 Now I urge you, brethren, by our Lord Jesus Christ and by *a*the love of the Spirit, to *b*strive together with me in your prayers to God for me,

31 that I may be *a*delivered from those who are disobedient in Judea, and *that* my *b*service for Jerusalem may prove acceptable to the *c*saints;

32 so that *a*I may come to you in joy by *b*the will of God and find *refreshing* rest in your company.

33 Now *a*the God of peace be with you all. Amen.

30 *a*Gal. 5:22; Col. 1:8 *b*2 Cor. 1:11; Col. 4:12

31 *a*2 Cor. 1:10; 2 Thess. 3:2; 2 Tim. 3:11; 4:17 *b*Rom. 15:25f.; 2 Cor. 8:4; 9:1 *c*Acts 9:13, 15

32 *a*Rom. 15:23 *b*Acts 18:21; Rom. 1:10

33 *a*Rom. 16:20; 2 Cor. 13:11; Phil. 4:9; 1 Thess. 5:23

Fig. 3.3

A. PRELIMINARY CHECKS

BOOK   The book is Romans—one of Paul's letters to Christians.

TYPE   Romans is a letter, so we can expect an epistolary style, with many personal notes and exhortations. Because it is a letter to a church, we can expect to read teaching of different kinds.

SETTING   A group of Christians has started a small
local church at Rome. Paul knows many of the people,
but he has not yet visited them at Rome. He wants to
instruct them about the doctrines of salvation, and to
encourage them in their walk with Christ.

PASSAGE   The passage (15:30-33) is the concluding
paragraph of the segment (15:14-33). It is Paul's testimony and tells of his plans, things he wants to share with
his readers toward the end of the letter.

Since this is a short passage, it will be possible to
examine it thoroughly in a devotional reading.

MN   There is only one marginal note shown in the
NASB, besides the many cross-references to other passages. The marginal note is for the translation "saints"
(v. 31) and refers the reader to the note for v. 25, which
says, "I.e., true believers; lit., *holy ones*."

QU   There are no quotes from the Old Testament.

BEF   The paragraphs before this report other testimonies and plans of Paul at that time.

AFT   The chapter that follows (16:1-27) concludes
the letter, mainly with greetings.

CON   The letter to the Romans closes with an epi-
logue of two kinds of personal notes:

Paul's Testimony and Plans (15:14-33)
Paul's Friends and Co-workers (16:1-27)

The paragraph of this devotional reading is the
conclusion of the first part.

B. EARLY OBSERVATIONS OF THE TEXT AND ITS STRUCTURE

(Whenever possible I will mark these in my Bible
with the pencil that's always in my hand.)

1. *Paragraph*. In preliminary checks I observed this passage as being the unit of a paragraph.

2. *Sentences*. I observe three sentences of different lengths. The first is long, involving three verses (30-32); the second is shorter—most of verse 33. The last is a one-word sentence, "Amen."

3. *Phrases*. Because the first sentence is long, it has many phrases. Of the longer ones, some begin with the word *by*:

"by our Lord Jesus Christ"
"by the love of the Spirit"
"by the will of God"

Others begin with the word *that*:

"that I may be delivered"
"that my service for Jerusalem may prove"
"that I may come to you"

There are many other shorter phrases, like:

"to God"
"in joy"

4. *Key or strong words*. Besides the references to Persons of the Godhead, these strong words stand out to me:

urge	disobedient
love	joy
strive	rest
prayers	peace
delivered	

5. *Other words*. The pronouns are prominent in this paragraph. The first person singular words are most frequent:

"I"—three times
"me"—two times
"my"—one time

6. *Conjunctions.* Conjunctions hold words and phrases together in long sentences like the first one of this paragraph. Connectives to look for are *and, but, because, as, since, when, for, therefore, after.* In this passage I observe *and* three times. This simple word is a clue to *lists* of things, which I want to keep in mind as I move on in my observing.

The word *but* is always important in a passage, because it introduces a contrasting thought. I do not observe it in this passage.

7. *Core.* I always look for the core of a long sentence. In this passage it is not hidden, and it appears early:
"I [main subject] URGE [main verb] YOU [main object]." Coming out of this main core is a secondary one: YOU (subject implied) STRIVE (verb) WITH ME (object). From this main core and its derivative comes this *overall thrust:* "I urge you to strive with me."

8. *Turning point.* I do not see a turning or pivotal point in the paragraph.

9. *Progression or climax.* There is an ongoing movement in the long sentence, leading to the climax, "find refreshing rest in your company" (v. 32).

C. TONE

The paragraph is a short one, but it has much feeling, partly explained by the fact that Paul is nearing the end of his letter. I sense a tone of urgency, borne out by the words "urge," "strive," and "be delivered." The passage concludes in an atmosphere of victory—which I feel when I read the words "joy," "rest," and "peace."

D. TALKING TEXT

1. I make more markings in the printed text of my Bible, especially to show emphasized and related words and phrases.

2. Then I recast the Bible text in my own way on a piece of paper, letting the text "talk." I always keep in mind that it is *emphases* and *relationships* that the talking text should reveal especially. The talking text may look something like that in figure 3.4.

Talking Text of Romans 15:30-33

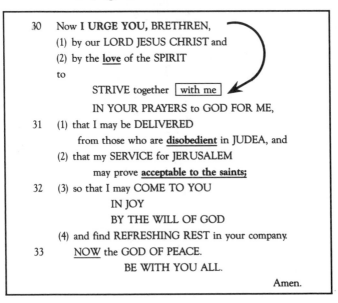

30   Now **I URGE YOU, BRETHREN,**
    (1) by our LORD JESUS CHRIST and
    (2) by the <u>love</u> of the SPIRIT
    to
        STRIVE together | with me |
        IN YOUR PRAYERS to GOD FOR ME,
31   (1) that I may be DELIVERED
        from those who are <u>disobedient</u> in JUDEA, and
    (2) that my SERVICE for JERUSALEM
        may prove <u>**acceptable to the saints;**</u>
32   (3) so that I may COME TO YOU
            IN JOY
            BY THE WILL OF GOD
    (4) and find REFRESHING REST in your company.
33   <u>NOW</u> the GOD OF PEACE.
        BE WITH YOU ALL.
                        Amen.

Fig. 3.4

3. This talking text will help me much in the "devotional search" that follows, which is the practical part of my devotional reading.

E. THE DEVOTIONAL "SEARCH"

Now I have come to the heart of my devotional reading of this passage, to see what it says about the

arena of life and how I am involved. This is the spiritual
exercise of my devotional reading. All that I have done
thus far has looked forward to this exercise. It may have
seemed like analytical study (and in some sense it was),
but it was all with the view to the *devotional search* I am
now embarking on.

I always keep in mind the diagram of the arena of
life (fig. 3.5).

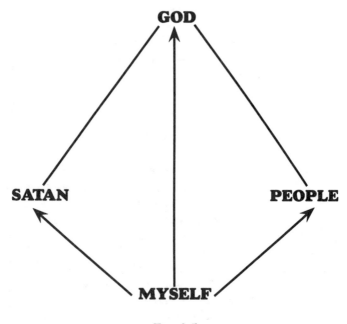

Fig. 3.5

1. *Arena observations.* The order of observing the
four points of the arena may vary from passage to passage. Here the order will be: MYSELF, PEOPLE, SA-
TAN, GOD. Note in the examples given below that
although this is the step of making *observations*, my
interpretations and applications are a natural outcome
of those. This instantaneous blend is a characteristic of
devotional reading.

MYSELF—To begin with, I identify with the believers of the church at Rome to whom Paul is writing this letter. Also, I can identify with Paul himself. Now I go through the text to see myself in it.

"brethren" (v. 30)—I am one of many spiritual brothers of the Lord's family.

"our Lord" (v. 30)—I am reminded that I am a servant of the Lord.

"together with me" (v. 30)—I am a fellow-worker with other believers.

"prayers . . . for me" (v. 30)—I can support other believers with intercessory prayer.

"my service for Jerusalem" (v. 31)—I should minister in service to other believers. (Here I am identifying with Paul.)

"the saints" (v. 31)—I am holy and set apart in Christ.

"refreshing rest in your company" (v. 32)—I should be part of a Christian fellowship that encourages witnesses of the gospel.

PEOPLE (the disobedient Judeans, cited below).

SATAN

"those who are disobedient in Judea" (v. 31)—These are enemies of the gospel. They are not believers; they do not obey the gospel. Satan is their master. Christians need to be delivered from their influence and opposition.

GOD

"our Lord Jesus Christ" (v. 30)—All true believers confess Jesus as Master, Savior, Messiah (Anointed One).

"love of the Spirit" (v. 30)—Love from the Holy Spirit is a powerful motivation to Christians.

"prayers to God" (v. 30)—Christians should strive in praying to God, believing that He wants them to pray to Him, and that He answers their prayers.

"come . . . by the will of God" (v. 32)—God has a will and plan for every part of a believer's life, including where he should be serving Him.

"God of peace" (v. 33)—God is the Author and Source of all peace in this sin-stricken world.

"be with you all" (v. 33)—God desires to dwell with His people, in their hearts.

Examples of *arena* observations in historical and poetic passages appear at the end of this chapter.

2. *Perspective.* I go back over the observations listed above to be sure that I have projected myself in this passage, for its spiritual help for my own life.

3. *Response and application.*

a) Responding with confession. Certain words and phrases remind me of sins that I may be guilty of, which I need to confess.

"prayers to God for me" (v. 30)—I confess I haven't been faithful in my intercessory prayer life.

"my service for Jerusalem" (v. 31)—My service in the work of the gospel and the local church is not what it should be. I get discouraged so easily, when I lose sight of Jesus.

"by the will of God" (v. 32)—Sometimes I get ahead of God, or make plans without thinking of *His* will for me.

b) Responding in faith.

Do I have utmost faith in the God of this passage? Do I believe that all of the Scripture is true?

Do I believe that the Scripture is intended to help me?

"love of the Spirit" (v. 30)—Do I believe that the Holy Spirit loves me and helps me serve the Lord as I should?

"prayers to God" (v. 30)—Do I *really* believe in the effectiveness of prayer?

"the will of God" (v. 32)—Just what do I believe about God's will for my life, as I live it day by day?

"God . . . be with you" (v. 33)—Have I ever spoken or written these words, or words like them, to someone? If so, did I share them in faith?

Do I think I have to understand every part of this Scripture in order to receive its help?

Have I asked the Spirit to help me apply this Scripture to my life?

c) Responding by obedience.

"those who are disobedient" (v. 31). These people were unbelievers but Christians can also be guilty of disobedience. If I have disobeyed my Lord in anything, I should confess the sin and promise to obey Him.

"I urge you . . . by our Lord Jesus Christ and by the love of the Spirit" (v. 30). What are my motives for obeying God? What are the incentives?

"strive together with me" (v. 30). Some saints, like Paul, leave good examples to follow. I need to obey what God is telling me through their examples:

I need to be zealous in Christian service as Paul was.

I need to feel for the needs of fellow believers and do things that will help them.

My fellow Christians need to see *joy* in my life.

The devotional search would conclude with recognizing any problem passage (e.g., what does it mean to

"strive" with a fellow believer in prayer to God?), spend-
ing a few minutes reflecting on all that I have been
experiencing in this devotional reading, and thanking
God for the Word He has given me.

F. TWO FURTHER EXAMPLES OF ARENA OBSERVATIONS

We would also like to illustrate the kinds of arena
observations that arise out of an Old Testament historical passage and out of a poetic passage. Prophetic passages of the Bible are basically the historical type—the
predictive parts are of history yet to be fulfilled.

The historical passage chosen is Exodus 3:1-12. The
poetic passage is Psalm 46. Psalms are excellent for devotional reading, because they are mainly songs of worship
and testimony that encourage reflection and meditation.

**Arena Observations of an
Old Testament Historical Passage**

Exodus 3:1-12 (NIV)

3 Now Moses was tending the flock of Jethro his father-in-law, the priest of
Midian, and he led the flock to the far side of the desert and came to Horeb,
the mountain of God. ²There the angel of the LORD appeared to him in flames
of fire from within a bush. Moses saw that though the bush was on fire it did
not burn up. ³So Moses thought, "I will go over and see this strange sight—why
the bush does not burn up."
⁴When the LORD saw that he had gone over to look, God called to him from
within the bush, "Moses, Moses!"
And Moses said, "Here I am."
⁵"Do not come any closer," God said. "Take off your sandals, for the place
where you are standing is holy ground." ⁶Then he said, "I am the God of your
father, the God of Abraham, the God of Isaac and the God of Jacob." At this,
Moses hid his face, because he was afraid to look at God.
⁷The LORD said, "I have indeed seen the misery of my people in Egypt. I have
heard them crying out because of their slave drivers, and I am concerned about
their suffering. ⁸So I have come down to rescue them from the hand of the
Egyptians and to bring them up out of that land into a good and spacious land,
a land flowing with milk and honey—the home of the Canaanites, Hittites,
Amorites, Perizzites, Hivites and Jebusites. ⁹And now the cry of the Israelites
has reached me, and I have seen the way the Egyptians are oppressing them.
¹⁰So now, go. I am sending you to Pharaoh to bring my people the Israelites
out of Egypt."
¹¹But Moses said to God, "Who am I, that I should go to Pharaoh and bring
the Israelites out of Egypt?"
¹²And God said, "I will be with you. And this will be the sign to you that
it is I who have sent you: When you have brought the people out of Egypt, you
will worship God on this mountain."

Fig. 3.6

GOD

"mountain of God" (v. 1)—I am reminded of God the Creator of all things.

"angel of the Lord appeared" (v. 2)—God the Lord is a miracle-worker, and He appears on this earth scene in different ways.

"God called to him" (v. 4)—God can speak to *anyone*.

"Do not come any closer. . . . holy ground" (v. 5)—God is holy.

"God of Abraham" (v. 6)—God is the Lord and Father of His chosen people.

"I have indeed seen. . . . I have heard" (v. 7)—God sees all and hears all.

"I am concerned" (v. 7)—God is compassionate.

"I have come down to rescue" (v. 8)—God is Savior.

"I am sending you" (v. 10)—God sovereignly commissions a person for His work.

"I will be with you" (v. 12)—God is at the side of His people.

"You will worship God" (v. 12)—God is to be worshiped.

SATAN

"do not come any closer" (v. 5)—The holy presence of God cannot be defiled by the sins of man.

"misery of my people" (v. 7)—The misery, crying, suffering, and oppression were inflicted on God's people by the idolatrous Egyptians (vv. 8-9).

"slave drivers" (v. 7)—Persecution is one of Satan's tools.

PEOPLE

"tending the flock of Jethro" (v. 1)—One of our most common contacts with other people is at our daily occupations.

"my people" (v. 7)—God has certain believers

whom He calls to special work, but He regards
no less highly the work of *all* His children. He
affectionately calls them "my people."

"Egyptians" (v. 8)—The world is always populated
by two kinds of people—believers and unbelievers. In this passage, most (if not all) of the Egyptians are unbelievers. Most of the Israelites are
believers at this time.

MYSELF—I identify myself with Moses and the Israelites.

"tending the flock" (v. 1)—I should never be lazy.

"why the bush does not burn up" (v. 3)—I can learn
much from asking "Why?"

"Here I am." (v. 4)—I should always respond to
God's voice.

"he was afraid to look at God" (v. 6)—I should
always fear God in reverence and awe of who He
is.

"the cry of the Israelites has reached me" (v. 9)—God
wants me to cry to Him for help, when I am in
need.

"Who am I?" (v. 11)—I should always be humble
before God.

"I will be with you" (v. 12)—I can count on God's
presence and help to do the work He commissions me to do.

"the sign . . . when you have brought the people
out of Egypt" (v. 12)—I should have faith that
God can and will fulfill what He promises to do.

GOD

"God is our refuge . . . strength . . . help"
(v. 1)—God is an ever-present help to His people.

"make glad the city of God" (v. 4)—God dwells in a
city of joy, with His people.

"the Most High" (v. 4)—God is over all (cf. v. 10).

Arena Observations of a Poetic Passage

Psalm 46 (NASB)

PSALM 46

God the Refuge of His People.

For the choir director. *A Psalm* of the sons of
Korah, [f]set to Alamoth.   A Song.

GOD is our [a]refuge and strength,
    [1]A very [b]present help [c]in [2]trouble.
2 Therefore we will [a]not fear, though [b]the earth should
    change,
    And though [c]the mountains slip into the heart of the
    [1]sea;
3 Though its [a]waters roar *and* foam,
    Though the mountains quake at its swelling pride.
                    [[1]Selah.

4 There is a [a]river whose streams make glad the [b]city of
    God,
    The holy [c]dwelling places of the Most High.
5 God is [a]in the midst of her, she will not be moved;
    God will [b]help her [1]when morning dawns.
6 The [1]nations [a]made an uproar, the kingdoms tottered;
    He [2b]raised His voice, the earth [c]melted.
7 The LORD of hosts [a]is with us;
    The God of Jacob is [b]our stronghold. ·   [Selah.

8 Come, [a]behold the works of the LORD,
    [1]Who has wrought [b]desolations in the earth.
9 He [a]makes wars to cease to the end of the earth;
    He [b]breaks the bow and cuts the spear in two;
    He [c]burns the chariots with fire.
10 "[1]Cease *striving* and [a]know that I am God;
    I will be [b]exalted among the [2]nations, I will be exalted
    in the earth."
11 The LORD of hosts is with us;
    The God of Jacob is our stronghold.   [Selah.

1 [1]Or, *Abundantly available for help* [2]Or, *tight places*
[a]Ps. 14:6; 62:7, 8 [b]Ps. 145:18; Deut. 4:7 [c]Ps. 9:9

2 [1]Lit., *seas*
[a]Ps. 23:4; 27:1 [b]Ps. 82:5 [c]Ps. 18:7

3 [1]*Selah may mean: Pause, Crescendo* or *Musical interlude*
[a]Ps. 93:3, 4; Jer. 5:22

4 [a]Ps. 36:8; 65:9; Is. 8:6; Rev. 22:1 [b]Ps. 48:1; 87:3; 101:8; Is. 60:14; Rev. 3:12 [c]Ps. 43:3

5 [1]Lit., *at the turning of the morning*
[a]Deut. 23:14; Is. 12:6; Ezek. 43:7, 9; Hos. 11:9; Joel 2:27; Zech. 2:5 [b]Ps. 37:40; Is. 41:14; Luke 1:54

6 [1]Or, *Gentiles* [2]Lit., *gave forth*
[a]Ps. 2:1, 2 [b]Ps. 18:13; 68:33; Jer. 25:30; Joel 2:11; Amos 1:2 [c]Amos 9:5; Mic. 1:4; Nah. 1:5

7 [a]Num. 14:9; 2 Chr. 13:12 [b]Ps. 9:9; 48:3

8 [1]Or, *Which He has wrought as desolations*
[a]Ps. 66:5 [b]Is. 61:4; Jer. 51:43

9 [a]Is. 2:4; Mic. 4:3 [b]Ps. 76:3; 1 Sam. 2:4 [c]Is. 9:5; Ezek. 39:9

10 [1]Or, *Let go, relax* [2]Or, *Gentiles*
[a]Ps. 100:3 [b]Is. 2:11, 17

Fig. 3.7

"God will help her when morning dawns" (v. 5)—
    God is always available to give help.

"He raised His voice, the earth melted" (v. 6)—God
    is omnipotent.

"Lord of hosts" (v. 7)—God has many servants and
    is over all.

"God of Jacob" (v. 7)—God is in special relation to
    Jews who are faith descendants of Jacob.

"works of the Lord" (v. 8)—God performs all kinds
of miracles (vv. 8-9).

SATAN

"trouble" (v. 1)—All trouble has its source in Satan.

"we will not fear" (v. 2)—This kind of fear comes
from unbelief.

"though the earth should change" (v. 2)—Catastrophes of the physical universe are traced back to
the Fall (Genesis 3).

"she will not be moved" (v. 5)—Satan desires to
harm the people of God, but God is their
stronghold.

"desolations in the earth" (v. 8)—These are divine
judgments for sin.

"wars" (v. 9)—All wars are traced back to Satan,
ultimately. Conflict, hate, and greed are satanic.

PEOPLE

"nations made an uproar" (v. 6)—The power of the
masses, under the flag of a nation, is awesome.

"He makes wars to cease" (v. 9)—People may fight
each other—God is sovereign over all.

"I will be exalted among the nations" (v. 10)—The
call goes out to all people: Will you receive and
worship God the Lord?

"The Lord of hosts is with us" (v. 11)—These are
people of God living throughout the world—the
Lord of hosts is always with them.

MYSELF—I identify with the believing psalmist, and
with the believers he writes about, whom he
identifies by the pronouns *we, our,* and *us.*

"we will not fear" (v. 2)—I can count on God's help
in all kinds of trouble—even catastrophe.

"whose streams make glad" (v. 4)—If I'm a citizen of
God's city, I should be a joyful one.

"God is in the midst of her" (v. 5)—Do I have this intimate fellowship with God?

"God will help her" (v. 5)—What kinds of help do I need?

"Come, behold the works of the Lord" (v. 8)—God wants me to behold His mighty works, so that my faith will increase.

"Cease striving and know that I am God" (v. 10)—For full knowledge of God I need to rest completely in faith in Him, exalting and glorifying Him.

4

The Activities of Analytical Reading

"Some books are to be tasted, others to be swallowed, and some few to be chewed and digested." Francis Bacon was referring to analytical reading when he said "chewed and digested." The Bible is a book to be read that way, in an analysis that is thorough and complete, not limited by time, and not for mere information or for entertainment. Devotional reading stresses the worship experience of the reader; informational reading stresses the gathering of vital information; analytical reading stresses the minute search and examination of all the parts of the Bible text. Analytical reading can be the most exciting experience you have in studying God's Word.

I. What Analytical Reading Is

The dictionary defines analysis as the separation of the whole into constituent parts for individual study. When analyzing the Bible, the range of study is from the whole unit (for example, a segment or paragraph) to the individual words that make up that unit. The procedure of analysis is of three steps, in this order:

OBSERVATION—What does the text say?
INTERPRETATION—What does that mean?
APPLICATION—How does this affect me?

Observation is the key activity of analytical reading, but interpretations and applications are also made, based on the observations. It is very difficult to distinguish between analytical reading and analytical study, because they are so similar. Analytical reading is part of analytical study. For this discussion we shall use the terms interchangeably, disregarding any technical differences.

A. AN EXPERIENCE OF METHODICAL STUDY

Method is simply orderly procedure. The orderliness of analytical reading is seen in these things about it:

1. It is always the reading of a *unit* of text, whether that is a verse, paragraph, segment, section, or the whole book. Most of the time it is the reading of a segment (group of paragraphs). This is symbolized by the logo:

The outer rectangle of the logo encloses the text of the whole segment, and this whole unit is divided here into three paragraphs of text.

2. It follows procedures and methods in a regular pattern of study.

3. It attempts to examine everything of the text, the word content and also the form (how the words were put together).

4. It aims at completion of the whole project.

Analytical reading is inductive in approach. That is, it lets the Bible text speak for itself. It can do nothing else, since it is only the Bible text that is read, not books or commentaries on the text. It is important for the reader not to make the text say what *he* wants it to say.

B. OBJECTIVES OF ANALYTICAL READING

The main objective of analytical reading is to make a thorough examination of all the parts of a unit of Scripture, as a basis for interpreting and applying it. As noted above, it does this by following the inductive approach of letting the Bible speak for itself. The ultimate objective of analytical reading is the application of the Bible text to the life of the reader. This should be true of all Bible reading.

II. Three Vital Mind-Sets

How effective your analytical reading is depends on a lot of factors, many of which arise out of the procedures to be described in the pages that follow. For now, keep in mind three important mind-sets:

A. VALUE THE SCRIPTURES

The esteem you have for the Bible text can make the difference between good and ineffective analytical reading. Try reading a Bible passage aloud, imagining that you are God's messenger reading it to your listeners for the first time. Which of the two following ways would you choose for reading this important message from God: (1) clear, slow, forceful diction, reciting each word and phrase interpretatively; or (2) overly fast, in a monotone, with no pauses and inflections, and with no feeling or meaning imparted to the words? Does this suggest to you something of the esteem and respect and awe that should fill your heart and mind as you read the Bible, silently or aloud? Every word is God's Word, and it is eternally important. Let your analytical reading show it.

B. CONCENTRATE

Analytical reading is the meticulous scrutiny and examination of all the parts of the Bible text, from large to small, including punctuation. It is no wonder that concentration is a must for effective reading. I have never heard a star athlete interviewed on radio or TV who hasn't recognized *concentration* as a major key to his success. Lanny Bassham, Olympic gold-medalist in small-bore rifle competition, tells what concentration does for his marksmanship:

> Our sport is controlled nonmovement. We are shooting from 50 meters—over half a football field—at a bull's-eye three-quarters the size of a dime. If the angle of error at the point of the barrel is more than .005 of a millimeter (that is five one-thousandths), you drop into the next circle and lose a point. So we have to learn how to make everything stop. I stop my breathing. I stop my digestion by not eating for 12 hours before the competition. I train by running to keep my pulse around 60, so I have a full second between beats—I have gotten it lower, but found that the stroke-volume increased so much that each beat really jolted me. You do all of this and you have the technical control. But you have to have some years of experience in reading conditions: the wind, the mirage. *Then you have the other 80% of the problems—the mind.*[1]

To be a winner, you have to discipline yourself to concentrate. Why not be a winner in analytical reading?

C. RELAX

When it comes to production and performance, it is an accepted fact that relaxation has a lot to do with maximum productivity. This doesn't cancel out concen-

---

1. Kenny Moore, "Enough to Take His Breath Away," *Sports Illustrated*, 2 August 1976, pp. 31-35. Emphasis added.

tration—it reinforces it. A value of relaxation is illustrated by another story from the sports world. The Philadelphia Phillies were losing 13-2 in the early innings of a baseball game with the Chicago Cubs. Mike Schmidt, home-run star of the Phillies, had mentally conceded a victory for the Cubs. So each time at bat he relaxed, swinging the bat like he was at batting practice. Outcome? He hit four home runs in the game, and the Phillies won, 18-16!

How can you relax when you are reading the Bible analytically? Try this: think of everything that is in your favor. You can't lose. Think what the Word is—for example, it is your spiritual food. Think what it can do for you—it can only help you, for whatever needs you have. And think of the matchless company you have with you—the One who wrote the Scripture text, and who is enlightening your spiritual eyes—the Holy Spirit. It is when you relax in reading that you begin to sense the great joy and satisfaction of learning what God has written to you.

III. Connections Between Reading and Recording

Recall the statement that "a pencil is one of the best eyes." Implied there is the fact that if you use a pencil as you read, you will see twice as much. Recording should go along with reading because it reaps such rich dividends.

What kinds of things should your pencil record on paper or on the pages of your Bible, as you read the text? Here are some suggestions:

- Your reactions (even the underlining of a word could express such responses as "Amen," surprise, awe, and attention)
- Your questions
- Your identifications of highlights of the passage
- Your observations of things emphasized
- Your observations of related things

Each recording you make has some kind of purpose, such as the following:

- To express reactions
- To summarize the unit
- To initiate and suggest later studies
- To make a permanent record

More will be said about recording in the pages that follow.

IV. Getting Things Ready

Of the three kinds of reading—devotional, analytical, informational—you will probably spend more time getting ready for analytical reading than for the other two kinds. Since we have already described and demonstrated preliminary checks in earlier pages, only a few notes will appear here.

A. PRELIMINARY CHECKS

BOOK   All books of the Bible wait to be analyzed. There is a variety of challenge, difficulty, and interest, depending on the type of book you choose.

TYPE   Some of the most stimulating analytical reading is done in doctrinal passages of the Bible, especially the New Testament. This is partly because so much interrelated doctrine is compacted in such small space.

SETTING   Where, when, and why did the book first appear? These are questions you want to answer before you make an analytical reading of one of its passages.

PASSAGE   For analytical reading, the best passages to use are paragraphs or segments. These units are neither too short (analysis usually calls for longer substantive units) nor too long (which would tend to make the project a survey rather than analysis). If the passage is a segment, note how it is broken down into paragraphs.

MN Scan your Bible's notes before reading the passage. Note any alternate readings that are supported by ancient manuscripts. (But keep in mind that the translators of your Bible have chosen the manuscript evidence behind the translation that appears in the regular printed text.) Compare how other versions translate these parts.

Read other notes in the margin, such as explanations or interpretations. Keep these in mind when you do the reading.

QU Note any quotation from the Old Testament. Read the Old Testament setting of the original text that is quoted. You will do more with this at a later time, if you analyze the text more closely.

BEF , AFT , and CON Read the paragraphs or segments before and after the passage, to catch the connections. What continuity do you see? The passage of your analytical reading will be seen to rest very nicely where it is when you have observed this continuity.

B. TEXT LAID OUT: THE STRUCTURE

Think of the passage you are about to read as a structure built of many parts, kept together by the author as one unit.

1. *Segment.* A segment is a group of paragraphs, recording one main subject. When you read the full segment, you are moving from the beginning of that subject to its last word. You should be able to state the

main subject in a few words. Also, it is usually possible to find a key word or phrase somewhere in the segment that represents the main subject.

Other things to be observed in a segment will be discussed later in this chapter.

The NIV, *Good News Bible*, and *Layman's Bible Study Notebook* are good sources for identifying where new segments begin.

2. *Paragraphs.* A paragraph is a group of sentences revolving around one main thought. Each paragraph represents one point under the main subject of the segment of which it is a part. Note on the text of Matthew 4:1-11 (fig. 4.1) how the paragraphs fall under the main subject.

Main Subject: Three Temptations of Jesus
Key Center: "tempted of the devil" (4:1)
Paragraph Points: 1. Food   4:1-4
                   2. Protection 4:5-7
                   3. Possessions 4:8-11

Refer to versions for help in identifying paragraph divisions. Often versions differ on where to begin a new paragraph, partly because of the transitional nature of some sentences. You may find it best to assign your own divisions, which isn't a difficult task. Figure 4.1 shows how NIV divides Matthew 4:1-11 into seven paragraphs, whereas the *Layman's Bible Study Notebook* divides it into three paragraphs.[2]

3. *Sentences.* Scan each paragraph for its sentences. Are the sentences long? short? simple? complex? factual? reflective? Are there any questions? exclamations? com-

2. The bullet (•) represents a paragraph division in the *Layman's Bible Study Notebook* (Eugene, Ore.: Harvest House, 1978). Note: verse 11 is a concluding verse of the segment, and may be considered a separate paragraph.

mands? quoted conversations? contrasts? lists? How do the opening sentences of the paragraphs compare?

Matthew 4:1-11 (NIV)

4 Then Jesus was led by the Spirit into the desert to be tempted by the devil. [2]After fasting forty days and forty nights, he was hungry. [3]The tempter came to him and said, "If you are the Son of God, tell these stones to become bread."

[4]Jesus answered, "It is written: 'Man does not live on bread alone, but on every word that comes from the mouth of God.'[a]" ●

[5]Then the devil took him to the holy city and had him stand on the highest point of the temple. [6]"If you are the Son of God," he said, "throw yourself down. For it is written:

" 'He will command his angels
        concerning you,
    and they will lift you up in their
        hands,
    so that you will not strike your foot
        against a stone.'[b]"

[7]Jesus answered him, "It is also written: 'Do not put the Lord your God to the test.'[c]" ●

[8]Again, the devil took him to a very high mountain and showed him all the kingdoms of the world and their splendor. [9]"All this I will give you," he said, "if you will bow down and worship me."

[10]Jesus said to him, "Away from me, Satan! For it is written: 'Worship the Lord your God, and serve him only.'[d]"

[11]Then the devil left him, and angels came and attended him. ●

(Fig. 4.1)

4. *Smaller but important parts.* Every part of the segment is vital, and this includes the phrases, words, and even punctuation. When you read the passage analytically, you must be aware that each individual part is *vital.*

a) Words. Really, words are the material, the *stuff,* of the Bible. Paul Leedy recognizes the function of words with this comparison:

"Words on the page are like red blood cells in the body. Both are carriers. As red corpuscles carry oxygen to the tissues, so words carry the thought of the writer to the mind of the reader."[3]

Be alert to the variety of kinds of words that may appear in the passage you are reading. Here are some kinds to look for (more kinds will be discussed later in the chapter):

(1) Connectives—conjunctions like *and, since, but*

(2) Figurative terms (discussed in chapter 2)

(3) Words that answer these questions: who, what, when, where, how, why

(4) Unusual, unexpected words

(5) Key words and strong words

(6) Bible subjects (some of the subjects appearing often in the Bible: God, Father, Son, Spirit, man, doctrines, salvation, belief and unbelief, Christian living, character, service, commands, exhortations, warnings, earth, world, heaven, hell, Satan, church, works of God, judgment)

b) Phrases. A phrase is a unit of two or more words expressing a brief thought. One of the best things you can do to improve your analytical reading is to train your eyes to read the Bible text *phrase by phrase*. Example: Read Romans 8:26 in your Bible, and observe the progression of these ten phrases:

And in the same way
    the Spirit also
    helps our weakness;

---

3. Paul D. Leedy, *Improve Your Reading* (New York: McGraw-Hill, 1956), p. 419.

> for we do not know
> how to pray
> as we should,
>
> but the Spirit Himself
> intercedes for us
> with groanings
> too deep for words.

When you are identifying phrases, always look for the *shortest* combination of words. Then later you may combine two short phrases into one long phrase (e.g., "how to pray as we should").

The importance of reading the Bible phrase by phrase will be seen later when we discuss the talking text.

c) Punctuation. Punctuation marks were not part of the original Bible autographs. They are added by the translators to help the reader. What specifically is that help? Paul Leedy answers this when he calls punctuation "the traffic lights of reading." Here is how he expands on this, in a very picturesque way:

The purpose of punctuation is to speed the reader on his way. . . . Punctuation aims to keep him out of traffic jams that occur when words follow too closely upon one another and when one thought swerves into the path of another thought without due warning or sufficient pause.

Words and thoughts are like city traffic: they need to be controlled if everything is to proceed smoothly and without interruption. Otherwise, ideas jam up, the reader becomes confused, and the whole verbal tangle results. . . .

Punctuation regulates the speed of reading. On a clear straightaway the reader is at liberty to breeze down the printways until a period brings him momentarily to a halt. Then with a new sentence, and a new spurt of power, he is off to the next thought's end.[4]

Read the following two passages of Hebrews. Note that each passage is one long sentence in the version used. How does punctuation help your reading and understanding of each unit?

Hebrews 1:1-4 (NKJV)

GOD, who at various times and in different ways spoke in time past to the fathers by the prophets,
2   has in these last days spoken to us by *His* Son, whom He has appointed heir of all things, through whom also He made the worlds;
3   who being the brightness of *His* glory and the express image of His person, and upholding all things by the word of His power, when He had by Himself[1] purged our[2] sins, sat down at the right hand of the Majesty on high,
4   having become so much better than the angels, as He has by inheritance obtained a more excellent name than they.

Fig. 4.2

Hebrews 2:2-4 (NKJV)

2   For if the word spoken through angels proved steadfast, and every transgression and disobedience received a just reward,
3   how shall we escape if we neglect so great a salvation, which at the first began to be spoken by the Lord, and was confirmed to us by those who heard *Him*,
4   God also bearing witness both with signs and wonders, with various miracles, and gifts of the Holy Spirit, according to His own will?

Fig. 4.3

4. Ibid., p. 106.

There are eleven points of punctuation in the English language, identified below. Their functions may seem obvious, but do not take them for granted. Let them alert you to the structure of the passage you are reading. Read the verses cited as examples.

(1) Period. A period is the reader's stop signal. Before going on to the next sentence, you may want to reread the sentence just completed. Bible versions differ on the lengths of sentences. Compare the following NIV readings of Hebrews 1:1-4 and 2:2-4 with the NKJV readings shown earlier. Compare the periods and commas of each.

Hebrews 1:1-4 (NIV)

1 In the past God spoke to our forefathers through the prophets at many times and in various ways, ²but in these last days he has spoken to us by his Son, whom he appointed heir of all things, and through whom he made the universe. ³The Son is the radiance of God's glory and the exact representation of his being, sustaining all things by his powerful word. After he had provided purification for sins, he sat down at the right hand of the Majesty in heaven. ⁴So he became as much superior to the angels as the name he has inherited is superior to theirs.

Fig. 4.4

Hebrews 2:2-4 (NIV)

²For if the message spoken by angels was binding, and every violation and disobedience received its just punishment, ³how shall we escape if we ignore such a great salvation? This salvation, which was first announced by the Lord, was confirmed to us by those who heard him. ⁴God also testified to it by signs, wonders and various miracles, and gifts of the Holy Spirit distributed according to his will.

Fig. 4.5

(2) Exclamation point (!)—This is like a period, but with more intensity and feeling.

(3) Semicolon (;)—A semicolon appears at the end of one thought, and indicates that a similar thought follows in that sentence. "He saved others; let Him save Himself" (Luke 23:35).

(4) Comma (,)—The comma is the most used of all punctuation points. Among its purposes are:

- to separate different points in a sentence
- to indicate lists
- to break down a long statement into shorter parts
- to introduce the statement that follows

Read the NKJV translation of the Hebrews passages again and see why the commas were used in these sentences.

(5) Colon (:)—A colon indicates that what follows is basically explanatory. "And since we have gifts . . . let each exercise them accordingly: if prophecy, according to the proportion of his faith" (Romans 12:6).

(6) Quotation marks (" ")—In the Bible these set off the quotes of another person or writing.

(7) Dash (—)—A set of dashes surrounds a parenthetical statement (see 1 Peter 3:21, NASB). A single dash indicates that what follows is an amplification of what has just appeared. "Therefore let all the house of Israel know for certain that God has made

Him both Lord and Christ—this Jesus whom you crucified" (Acts 2:36).

(8) Parentheses ( )—Parentheses include material that is easily detachable from the sentence (Ephesians 5:9).

(9) Brackets ([ ])—The words between brackets are inserted by another author. NASB uses this sparingly, in a special way (for example, surrounding John 7:53—8:11).

(10) Question mark (?) There are different kinds of questions, but only one question mark.

(11) Ellipses (. . .)—Usually these three periods represent something that has been left out. This form of punctuation does not appear in the Bible, but it is often used when Scripture is quoted elsewhere.

C. TONE

As noted earlier it is very important to feel the tone and atmosphere of the passage you are reading. This can be a valuable clue to what the Bible author is getting across. Among the questions to ask is, "How did the author feel when he wrote this?"

V. Focus on the Full Text

We have been discussing a number of things that go into preparation for analytical reading of a Bible passage. We saw the values of concentration, relaxation, and the recording of our observations. We were reminded again of the preliminary checks that precede reading, and we learned the importance of viewing the structure of the passage. Now before we focus on the full text, a few more things need to be said:

1. We have been using the singular phrase "analytical reading," but in reality there is no such thing as *one*

analytical reading of a passage. The very process of analysis calls for many readings.

2. Remember that in your reading there should always be the coactivity of *discovering* and *reading*. As you read, look for things; be alert to everything, including the unexpected; look peripherally—for example, as you read verse 5 in a passage keep glancing back at the verses just before it. And take pauses in your reading, to reflect on what you have just read, and to compare it with what may come up in the next lines.

Search can be exciting!

3. The following descriptions, and then the first example, will focus on the unit of one paragraph. The second example will involve a full segment.

4. Don't forget in your analytical reading to always keep a pencil in hand.

A. OVERRULING PATTERN: PHRASE BY PHRASE

Mark 5:25-29 (NASB)

25 And a woman who had had a hemorrhage for twelve years,

26 and had endured much at the hands of many physicians, and had spent all that she had and was not helped at all, but rather had grown worse,

27 after hearing about Jesus, came up in the crowd behind *Him*, and touched His [1]cloak.

28 For she [1]thought, "If I just touch His garments, I shall [2]get well."

29 And immediately the flow of her blood was dried up; and she felt in her body that she was healed of her [a]affliction.

Fig. 4.6

First read the paragraph of Mark 5:25-29 (fig. 4.6) in one short viewing, following the punctuation as you read. Then read it more slowly, phrase by phrase. You may want to underline some of the key phrases, for whatever reason.

Note that some phrases (and one word) are broken up by the right margin of the printed text. This is one of the biggest weaknesses of the printed text of Bibles. For example, note how much meaning is lacking because of the breakups in this paragraph:

v. 25   for twelve
v. 26   many physi-
v. 27   behind
v. 28   I shall

Your alert phrase-by-phrase reading can correct this shortcoming.

B. EMPHASES AND RELATIONSHIPS

Two key things to look for in any Bible passage are emphases and relationships. They are vital clues to what message the Bible author is trying to communicate. We discussed this briefly in connection with devotional reading, but more may be said now.

1. *Emphases.* The author emphasizes things in different ways.

a) Repetitions. Repeated or similar words and phrases are one of the best clues of emphasis. Do you see any in this paragraph?

b) Key words and phrases. This paragraph has many of these, for example, "spent all," "hearing about Jesus," "touch," "immediately."

c) Strong terms and other important words. These may not always be key words, but they are an important part of the story: for example "twelve years," "in the crowd," "felt in her body."

d) Feeling. What is the tone of the paragraph? How prominent is it?

e) Core of a long sentence. The Bible author would not have written a long sentence if he was not emphasizing something in it. But how do you catch that "something"? By identifying the core. The core of a sentence is the combination of main subject, main verb, and main object. For example, watch how the two-verse sentence of Hebrews 7:1-2 is organized:

"For THIS MELCHIZEDEK,
   (1) king of Salem,
   (2) priest of the MOST HIGH GOD,
   (3) who met ABRAHAM as he was
                 returning from the slaughter
                 of the kings and blessed him,
   (4) to whom also ABRAHAM apportioned
                 a tenth part of all the spoils,
   WAS   first of all,
            by the translation of his
            name,
   KING   of *righteousness*,
            and then also
   KING   of Salem, which is
   KING   of *peace*."

Note how the various descriptions are wrapped around this core:

main subject: THIS MELCHIZEDEK
main verb: WAS
main object: KING

(The full main object is a double one: king of righteousness, and king of peace.)

2. *Relationships.* One of the distinctive features of Scripture is the unique interrelatedness of all its parts.

This does not surprise us, because the Bible has one central message, and it communicates this in a multitude of ways. As you read a passage of the Bible, watch how its different parts are related to each other. This will give you many insights into what the author is communicating. Here are some kinds of relationships to look for:

a) Lists. The author doesn't list these by number. You must see them as you read the text. Some lists are short; others long. Here are some kinds:

things: "there is a lad here, who has
          (1) five barley loaves, and
          (2) two fish" (John 6:1-15)
names: "for I too am
          (1) an Israelite,
          (2) a descendant of Abraham,
          (3) of the tribe of Benjamin"
          (Romans 11:1)
actions: "and (1) had endured much . . .
          and (2) had spent all" (Mark 5:26)
descriptions: "(1) the flow of her blood was
          dried up; and
          (2) she felt in her body that she
          was healed" (Mark 5:29)
doctrines: "and we (1) have believed
          and (2) have come to know"
          (John 6:69)

b) Comparisons. Bible authors are always making comparisons, whether by likeness or contrast. The comparisons may be of things within a verse, or of words and phrases that are far apart (for example, at the beginning and end of a segment or paragraph). Here are examples:
Likeness—"was *not helped* at all,
          but rather had *grown worse*" (Mark 5:26)

Contrast—Notice how the first and last lines of
Mark 5:25-29 are contrasted:
"had a *hemorrhage*"
"*healed* of her affliction"

c) Cause and effect. There are many portions of
Scripture that bring out this divine principle of
God's creation. Note the cause and effect in
Mark 5:28: "If I just touch His garments, I shall
get well." What do you identify as cause and
effect in this statement: "God causes all things to
work together for good to those who love God"
(Romans 8:28)? What about this phrase: "having
now been justified by His blood" (Romans 5:9)?

d) Turning points. Sometimes in a segment or
paragraph the narrative or exposition makes a
definite turnabout. In Mark 5:25-29, the key
phrase responsible for the turnabout is, "after
hearing about Jesus" (5:27). The passage of Saul's
conversion (Acts 9:1-9) has a turning point at
verse 3, at the opening words, "And it came
about." Read the story of Jesus' crucifixion in
Matthew 27:33-56. In what sense is verse 50 a
turning point in the story?

e) Progression and climax. Observe the progression
and climax in the story of the woman:

(1) Beginning of the twelve-year illness
(2) Much endurance
(3) Many physicians
(4) Spent all
(5) Instantaneous healing—"immediately" (v. 29)

Usually the Bible author shows a progression in
the passage he is writing, without saying it in so
many words. Mark 1:14-28 shows among other

things the authority of Jesus in His public ministry. His authority is seen in His preaching (vv.
14-15); in His calling disciples (vv. 16, 20); in
teaching the multitude (vv. 21-22); in His rebuk-
ing and healing (vv. 25-26). The last two verses
of the passage report two big climaxes:

> "They were all amazed. . . . What is this? A
> new teaching with authority!" (1:27)
> "Immediately the news about Him went out
> everywhere" (1:28)

To summarize, when you are reading a passage analytically, look for *emphasized* things and *related* things.
You will find these to be the best indicators of what the
author is saying.

C. TALKING TEXT

We looked briefly at talking texts[5] in the chapter
on devotional reading. Now it's important to devote
more time to it, since it can be a very effective part of
your analytical reading. The objective of a talking text is
to show on paper (or vocally, in an oral reading) *what*
God wrote (content) and *how* He wrote it, especially by
emphases and relationships (form).

A comparison of the printed Bible text and a talking text will serve to describe what a talking text is (fig.
4.7). The printed text in your Bible runs from margin to
margin and, except for italicized words which represent
words not in the biblical manuscripts, the print is very
uniform. The small letter, without embellishments, is
the common type of print used, except for the first
word of a sentence, for proper names, or for occasional
entire words (e.g., LORD), when capital letters are used.
Indentations are seldom used for anything other than
the beginning of new paragraphs, for quotations of

---

5. Another name for talking text is textual recreation.

Scripture, or for the usual poetical structure. In other words, the format of the printed text in the Bible is rather homogeneous.

In the talking text, on the other hand, various graphic devices are used to indicate the actual grammatical and thought structure of a scriptural passage. That involves relations of words to words, relations of clauses to clauses, cores of sentences, distinctions between primary and subordinate phrases, listings of items, comparisons, turning points, progressions, key words, and phrases.

Among the various graphic aids you can use on paper to show the above structural items, emphases, and relationships are the following:

indentations	various colors
underlinings	arrows
large and small	numerical listings
capitalizations	blank spaces
small-type letters	color shading
circling, boxing	

Some of the above markings were applied to the Mark 5:25-29 passage, to make the accompanying partly-completed talking text. Note how the talking text compares with a regular NASB printing, especially as to phrase pattern.

Mark 5:25-29 (NASB)

25 And a woman who had had a hemorrhage for twelve years, 26 and had endured much at the hands of many physicians, and had spent all that she had and was not helped at all, but rather had grown worse, 27 after hearing about Jesus, came up in the crowd behind *Him,* and touched His cloak. 28 For she thought, "If I just touch His garments, I shall get well." 29And immediately the flow of her blood was dried up; and she felt in her body that she was healed of her affliction.

Partly Completed Talking Text of Mark 5:25-29 (NASB)

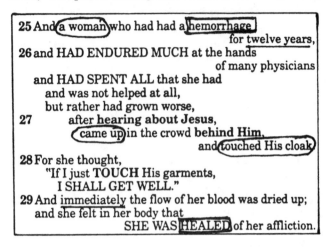

25 And a woman who had had a hemorrhage
                                    for twelve years,
26 and HAD ENDURED MUCH at the hands
                            of many physicians
   and HAD SPENT ALL that she had
      and was not helped at all,
      but rather had grown worse,
27   after hearing about Jesus,
         came up in the crowd behind Him,
                        and touched His cloak
28 For she thought,
      "If I just TOUCH His garments,
       I SHALL GET WELL."
29 And immediately the flow of her blood was dried up;
   and she felt in her body that
                    SHE WAS HEALED of her affliction.

Fig. 4.7

Here are a few practical suggestions for recording your own talking text on paper. This exercise is intimately involved with analytical reading (though not required), because repeated reading is involved. The procedure takes time, but it is amply rewarding, because of the concentration and reflection on the Bible text that goes along with the recording process.

1) Mark your Bible freely in a first reading, *anticipating textual recreation.*

2) You will not know how your final talking text will look before you begin. It is a growing process, open to change and revision.

3) Use scratch paper for your first talking text. Your ultimate goal is to do a final textual recreation on the first run.

4) Draw a rectangle (paragraph box) in which you will print the Bible text phrase by phrase.

5) General pattern: in your printing, move from left to right (phrase by phrase) and line by line.

6) Don't overdo any one graphic aid (e.g., underlining).

7) Use the whole paragraph box.
8) Don't *divide* a phrase (e.g., at the end of a line). *Be phrase-conscious.*
9) Keep the purpose of textual recreation in mind:

to show $\begin{cases} \text{EMPHASES} \\ \text{RELATIONSHIPS} \end{cases}$ clearly and forcefully

D. ORGANIZATION AND THEME OF THE PASSAGE

By this time it should be clear to you from the activities of your analytical readings what the passage's theme is, and how the author has composed the passage in his book. It will be helpful to you to write out the theme in your own words.

E. ORAL READING

If you have not done it already, read the passage aloud. It will amaze you how new vistas are opened as you hear your own voice speaking words and sentences you may never have voiced before. When you read, read interpretatively, with meaning and feeling. If you have recorded a talking text, read from it.

F. MEMORIZATION

A gratifying by-product of analytical reading is its aid in the direction of memorizing a passage. Because analytical reading requires repeated readings, concentration, assimilation, understanding of the passage, and feel for its tones, the reader is well on his way to memorizing the text. It can be seen how the talking text helps here, because the memorizer is able to visualize the progression of the Bible text as he has recorded it in the paragraph boxes.

G. APPLICATIONS

This is the highest point of your analytical reading. It is the time for the decisions you make on the basis of

what you observed in the Bible text and how you inter-
preted it. What those decisions and commitments are
depends much on your confidence in the Scriptures.
Always keep this in mind: The Bible is either true or it
is not true. If you reject it as untrue, you are rejecting its
claims and its Author, God. Then what are you left
with?

If you accept the Bible to be true, without reserva-
tion, then you must respond to its message. Recall what
you studied earlier about making applications from devotional reading, based on arena observations. Make the
same applications from your analytical reading. The following discussion is added here to help you make those
arena observations and applications, depending on
where in the Bible the passage of your reading is.

It is not difficult to know how to apply a simple
command like "Do all things without grumbling or dis-
puting" (Philippians 2:14). But can spiritual lessons be
derived from other types of passages, such as, "David
gave orders to gather the foreigners who were in the
land of Israel, and he set stonecutters to hew out stones
to build the house of God" (1 Chronicles 22:2)?

A key to this step of *application* is to recognize
where in the scheme of the Bible the passage is located,
and what kind of writing it is. Any Bible passage you
may read has a location in the diagram in figure 4.8.

Old Testament passages are prior to Christ, thus
many of them are of a Messianic nature. All New Testament passages following the gospels were written on the
basis of the death and resurrection of Christ as accom-
plished fact.

1. *When you are in the Old Testament.* Is the passage
one of *laws?* First determine how this might relate to
Christ—then involve yourself. For example, the burnt
offering of Leviticus 1:3 is a "male without defect"; the
offerer shall offer it "that he may be accepted before the
Lord." In its present application, Christ is the sacrifice
"without defect," and you as a Christian, in an act of

consecration, identify yourself with Christ that you may be accepted by God.

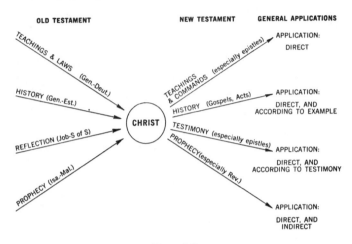

OLD TESTAMENT   NEW TESTAMENT   GENERAL APPLICATIONS

TEACHINGS & LAWS (Gen.-Deut.)

HISTORY (Gen.-Est.)

REFLECTION (Job-S of S)

PROPHECY (Isa.-Mal.)

CHRIST

TEACHINGS & COMMANDS (especially epistles)

HISTORY (Gospels, Acts)

TESTIMONY (especially epistles)

PROPHECY (especially Rev.)

APPLICATION: DIRECT

APPLICATION: DIRECT, AND ACCORDING TO EXAMPLE

APPLICATION: DIRECT, AND ACCORDING TO TESTIMONY

APPLICATION: DIRECT, AND INDIRECT

Fig. 4.8

Is the passage one of *history?* Again, the events might point forward to Christ, such as the exodus from Egypt as a type of the redemption of a sinner from the bondage of Satan. In any event, the *example* of how to approach God and live acceptably to Him appears throughout Old Testament history. Abraham's journey to the land of Canaan (Genesis 12:1-4) shows faith and obedience in action. Paul applied history like this in the following way: "these things happened to them as an example, and they were written for our instruction" (1 Corinthians 10:11).

Is the passage one of *testimony, prayer,* or *reflection,* such as is found in the poetic and wisdom literature? It is not difficult to make applications here, for the experiences of people are universal—we were all created alike, and we are all sinners in need of the same Savior. Psalm 51, the moving penitential prayer of David, is an example of Scripture that is personally applicable every day of our lives.

If the Scripture passage you are reading is one of

prophecy, you are reminded that God is an omniscient Designer and Sovereign Master of history. Regardless of what the prophecy is about, reading Bible prophecy should stir within your heart an increased devotion and faith in your God and Savior. If the Old Testament prophecy has been fulfilled, such as the death of Christ foretold in Isaiah 53, apply the passage to your life in view of the event's accomplishment. If the prophecy is yet to be fulfilled, such as the Lord's coming and the Great Tribulation foretold by Daniel, respond fervently to the reminder of the urgency of the days in which you are living.

The key to discovering the application of a Bible passage, especially in the Old Testament, is to derive the universal, timeless principle involved in the temporally-bound account. In studying such a biblical passage, the local temporal detail must first be identified. "Achan . . . took some of the things under the ban, therefore the anger of the Lord burned against the sons of Israel" (Joshua 7:1). The story goes on to relate that Israel lost heart and thirty-six men were slain—all because of one man's sin. Such was the local event of that moment. A timeless universal principle to be derived from the story is that the sin of one man in a group is bound to affect the whole group adversely.

2. *When you are in the New Testament.* The New Testament is usually easier to apply than the Old Testament, mainly because we are living in the same age as its writers and original readers. The applications themselves are generally the same as for the Old Testament, since the same *kinds* of writings make up the New Testament:

a) Teachings and commands—found especially in the epistles. Applications are usually direct, clear, and timeless. For example, "Let us love one another" (1 John 4:7).

b) History—mainly the gospels and Acts. Many kinds of applications can be made here, including:

- joys of following and serving Jesus
- daily walk of faith and prayer
- sins to avoid and examples to follow
- believing and appropriating what the Holy Spirit can do in your life
- impact of eternity, including judgment and reward

The passage we have just been studying (Mark 5:25-29) is in this history section. Do you see the kinds of applications you can make?

c) Testimony—found especially in the epistles. As a true Christian you can join in heart with the New Testament writers whenever you read a testimony such as Paul's "I know whom I have believed and I am convinced that He is able to guard what I have entrusted to Him until that day" (2 Timothy 1:12).

d) Prophecy—found throughout the New Testament, but especially in Revelation. Studying prophecy increases your faith, inspires service in the gospel to lost souls, and is an incentive to righteous living. Peter said, "Since all these things are to be destroyed in this way, what sort of people ought you to be in holy conduct and godliness, looking for and hastening the coming of the day of God?" (2 Peter 3:11-12).

Personal application of the Bible becomes an easier task and a more natural habit when we are convinced that the Bible offers up-to-date instruction, that it concerns us personally, and that its spiritual lessons are not hazy or ambiguous.

VI. Analytical Reading of a Paragraph

John 4:39-42 (NASB)

¶39   And from ᵃthat city many of the Samaritans believed in Him because of the word of the woman who testified, "ᵇHe told me all the things that I *have* done."
40   So when the Samaritans came to Him, they were asking Him to stay with them; and He stayed there two days.
41   And many more believed because of His word;
42   and they were saying to the woman, "It is no longer because of what you said that we believe, for we have heard for ourselves and know that this One is indeed ᵃthe Savior of the world."

39 ᵃJohn 4:5, 30 ᵇJohn 4:29

42 ᵃMatt. 1:21; Luke 2:11; John 1:29; Acts 5:31; 13:23; 1 Tim. 4:10; 1 John 4:14

Fig. 4.9

PRELIMINARY CHECKS

Of the complete set of preliminary checks that would normally be made, only the items of *before, after, and continuity* are illustrated here.

BEF   At 4:5 John reports the arrival of Jesus at a city of Samaria called Sychar. He ministers to a woman at Jacob's well, who is so impressed by what she hears that she tells the people of the city about it (4:7-30). The outcome of her sharing is the record of our passage, 4:39-42. The paragraph immediately preceding it (4:31-38) reports Jesus' instructions to His disciples about the harvest of souls, a harvest that is then wonderfully illustrated in the reading passage.

AFT   The next paragraph (4:43-45) reports Jesus leaving Sychar and traveling north to Galilee. I may conclude that 4:39-42 is the happy conclusion to the story of Jesus and the Samaritan woman.

CON   We can divide chapter 4 into three segments:
4:1-26   Jesus and a Samaritan woman
4:27-42   Further witness to Samaritans
4:43-54   Jesus' second miracle in Galilee

TEXT LAID OUT: THE STRUCTURE

Segment and paragraph. I read 4:27-42 as a segment, partly because the picture changes at verse 43.

The segment breaks down clearly into three paragraphs:

4:27-30   Woman's testimony
4:31-38   Jesus' teaching
4:39-42   Samaritans' conversions

From now on I will focus on the last paragraph, 4:39-42.

Sentences. The sentences of 4:39-42 are of varying lengths. Verse 42 could be viewed as a new sentence. If so, it would make verse 41 stand out boldly.

Phrases and words. Most of the phrases and words are plain, narrative vocabulary.

Punctuation. There are two sets of quotations (vv. 39, 42). The shorter statement was spoken by the woman; the longer, by the converted Samaritans.

I've observed earlier that the semicolon of verse 41 could be a period. But the semicolon *does* serve the purpose of closely relating verse 42 to verse 41. I'll want to look more into that later.

TONE OF THE PARAGRAPH

I read the entire paragraph again, as one unit, to *feel* its tone and atmosphere. Certain words set a tone of enthusiasm. These words include "many," "all the things," "many more believed," "indeed."

FOCUS ON THE FULL TEXT

Phrases. I read the NASB text *phrase by phrase*, aloud. Here are the phrases of the first line:
"from that city"

"many of the Samaritans"
"believed in"

I note that the NASB text breaks up the last phrase after the word "in" because the printer reached the margin at that point. Of course I will keep the full phrase intact, even though the printed text doesn't do so.

Sometimes I combine two phrases into one. Example: "we have heard for ourselves" (v. 42). Sometimes, for emphasis, it helps to keep a one-word phrase by itself. Example: "know" (v. 42).

Pauses. Long pauses are natural after verse 39 and verse 40. At the end of verse 39 I wonder if the people asked questions of the woman, and if so, what. At the end of verse 40 I wonder what kinds of things Jesus did for those two days, besides talking.

Inflections. I read the paragraph aloud again. There are no parentheses in the paragraph. In the woman's testimony (v. 39), I emphasize the phrase "all the things." In the Samaritans' testimony I raise my voice over "you" and "for ourselves." And I read with the tone of firmness and assurance the words "know" and "indeed."

The printed text does not have an exclamation point at the end of verse 42, but I read the last line as though it did.

EMPHASES AND RELATIONSHIPS.

Emphases:
1. repeated words: "believe(d)," "word," "woman," "because"
2. other key words and phrases: "stay with them," "heard for ourselves," "indeed," "Savior of the world"
3. feeling: prominent tone of assurance at end of paragraph

Relationships:

1. no formal lists in the text
2. comparisons: "word of the woman"→"His word"
3. cause and effect: "He stayed there two days"→ "many more believed"
4. turning point: "He stayed there two days" (Whatever it was that He did, it made a difference!)
5. progression: begins with "we have heard for ourselves"

Talking text. Now I record the Bible text, phrase by phrase, on paper in such a way that it will show these emphases and relationships (and other things) as a talking text. I will record the arrows and lines later.

Talking Text of John 4:39-42 (NASB)

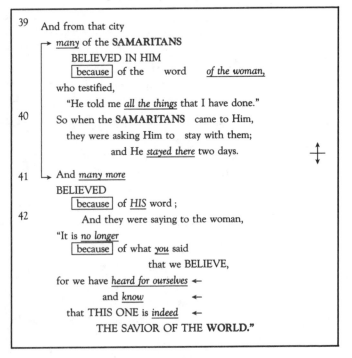

Fig. 4.10

Emphases shown on talking text:

1) I make the repeated words "BELIEVED" stand out, by size and location. (Throughout the Bible, "believe" is a key word.)
2) I block the word "because"—it appears three times, and has much to do with the paragraph's theme.
3) I circle the repeated word "word," also important in the passage.
4) I show the repetition of the word "SAMARITANS." (It was a "bad" word to orthodox Jews!)

Relationships shown on talking text:

1) The combination of "many" and "many more" reveals an increase. I connect these by an arrow. The explanation for the increase is seen in the phrase, "because of His word."
2) I show a relationship between the words "SAMARITANS" and "THE WORLD." Jesus is Savior of *all* who believe.
3) I draw a line between the phrases "word of the woman" and "His word." The story revolves around this comparison.
4) I show by arrows that there is a turning point at the last line of verse 40: "He stayed there two days."
5) I show by three arrows the ongoing progression of the phrases,
       "heard for ourselves"
       "know"
       "indeed"
   They powerfully lead up to the last line, which is the climax of the paragraph: THE SAVIOR OF THE WORLD. I print that climactic phrase large, and I color it.

Theme of the passage. My reading leads me to state the theme thus: The Sychar woman's testimony leads many Samaritans to believe in Christ, and many more believe Him because of the Word *He* instructs them.

Applications.

1) Jesus is the Savior of the world. I should consider everyone as those for whom He came to die.
2) True testimony about the Lord, from whatever source, can lead sinners to Christ. I should be a faithful witness of Christ, pointing sinners to Him.
3) Christ's testimony of Himself is very powerful in converting sinners. My testimony has its shortcomings, but I can ask Him to speak to hearts in His perfect and attracting way. I must share His Word with them.
4) Christ responds to the appeals of sinners to teach them the truth. I should never refuse to speak to someone who wants to hear about Jesus.

PRELIMINARY CHECKS

BOOK I have chosen Paul's letter to the church at Rome.

TYPE The book is epistolary, including much doctrine and quite a bit of testimony.

SETTING Paul wrote this letter toward the end of his third missionary journey, around A.D. 56. He has experienced many hardships up until now for his Christian witness, and he cannot expect this to let up.

PASSAGE The passage I have chosen is 8:28-39. NIV shows this to be a segment unit of study. I will use paragraph divisions at verses 28, 31, and 35.

VII. Analytical Reading of a Segment

Romans 8:28-39 (NASB)

28   And we know that ¹God causes ²all things to work together for good to those who love God, to those who are ᵇcalled according to *His* purpose.

29   For whom He ²foreknew, He also ᵇpredestined *to become* ᶜconformed to the image of His Son, that He might be the ᵈfirst-born among many brethren;

30   and whom He ²predestined, these He also ᵇcalled; and whom He called, these He also ᶜjustified; and whom He justified, these He also ᵈglorified.

¶31   ²What then shall we say to these things? ᵇIf God *is* for us, who *is* against us?

32   He who ²did not spare His own Son, but ᵇdelivered Him up for us all, how will He not also with Him freely give us all things?

33   Who will bring a charge against ²God's elect? ᵇGod is the one who justifies;

34   who is the one who ²condemns? Christ Jesus is He who ᵇdied, yes, rather who was ¹ᶜraised, who is ᵈat the right hand of God, who also ᶜintercedes for us.

35   Who shall separate us from ²the love of ¹Christ? Shall ᵇtribulation, or distress, or ᶜpersecution, or ᶠfamine, or ᵍnakedness, or ᶜperil, or sword?

36   Just as it is written,

"²FOR THY SAKE WE ARE BEING PUT TO DEATH ALL DAY LONG;

WE WERE CONSIDERED AS SHEEP TO BE SLAUGHTERED."

37   But in all these things we overwhelmingly ²conquer through ᵇHim who loved us.

38   For I am convinced that neither ²death, nor life, nor ᵇangels, nor principalities, nor ᶜthings present, nor things to come, nor powers,

39   nor height, nor depth, nor any other created thing, shall be able to separate us from ²the love of God, which is ᵇin Christ Jesus our Lord.

28 ¹Some ancient mss. read *all things work together for good*
ᵃRom. 8:32 ᵇRom. 8:30; 9:24; 11:29; 1 Cor. 1:9; Gal. 1:6, 15; 5:8; Eph. 1:11; 3:11; 2 Thess. 2:14; Heb. 9:15; 1 Pet. 2:9; 3:9

29 ᵃRom. 11:2; 1 Cor. 8:3; 2 Tim. 1:9; 1 Pet. 1:2, 20 ᵇRom. 9:23; 1 Cor. 2:7; Eph. 1:5, 11 ᶜ1 Cor. 15:49; Phil. 3:21; ᵈCol. 1:18; Heb. 1:6

30 ᵃRom. 9:23; 11:29; 1 Cor. 2:7; Eph. 1:5, 11 ᵇRom. 8:28; 9:24; 1 Cor. 1:9; Gal. 1:6, 15; 5:8; Eph. 1:11; 3:11; 2 Thess. 2:14; Heb. 9:15; 1 Pet. 2:9; 3:9 ᶜ1 Cor. 6:11 ᵈJohn 17:22; Rom. 8:21; 9:23

31 ᵃRom. 3:5; 4:1 ᵇPs. 118:6; Matt. 1:23

32 ¹John 3:16; Rom. 5:8 ᵇRom. 4:25

33 ᵃLuke 18:7 ᵇIs. 50:8f.

34 ¹Some ancient mss. read *raised from the dead* ᵃRom. 8:11 ᵇRom. 5:6f. ᶜActs 2:24 ᵈMark 16:19 ᶜRom. 8:27; Heb. 7:25

35 ¹Some ancient mss. read *God* ᵃRom. 8:37f. ᵇRom. 2:9; 2 Cor. 4:8 ᶜ1 Cor. 4:11; 2 Cor. 11:26f.

36 ᵃPs. 44:22; Acts 20:24; 1 Cor. 4:9; 15:30f.; 2 Cor. 1:9; 4:10f.; 6:9; 11:23

37 ᵃJohn 16:33; 1 Cor. 15:57 ᵇGal. 2:20; Eph. 5:2; Rev. 1:5

38 ᵃ1 Cor. 3:22 ᵇ1 Cor. 15:24; Eph. 1:21; 1 Pet. 3:22 ᶜ1 Cor. 3:22

39 ᵃRom. 5:8 ᵇRom. 8:1

Fig. 4:11

MN   Most of the marginal notes of NASB are cross-reference Scriptures. The notes particularly useful for my analytical reading are the alternate readings in these verses:

v. 28 "all things work together for good," for "God causes all things to work together for good"
v. 35 "God" for "Christ"

QU   Verse 36 quotes Psalm 44:22. The quote illustrates the fact of persecution just stated in verse 35.

BEF   The preceding paragraph (8:26-27) shows the Spirit helping Christians in their weaknesses.

AFT   The next three chapters (9, 10, 11) are about a new subject—God's sovereign ways with Israel.

CON   So 8:28-39 is the concluding passage of the Christian life section, chapters 6-8.

TEXT LAID OUT: THE STRUCTURE

Segment and paragraphs. I read the passage again, at a moderate speed. The segment is of three paragraphs, approximately equal in length. They form a unit around the common theme of the help of God.

Sentences. I scan the segment, to note the lengths of the sentences. There are two extra-long sentences: verses 29-30 and verses 38-39.

Phrases and words. The first paragraph has many doctrinal words, for example, "predestined." This is a contrast to the paragraph that follows, where the same kinds of truth are expressed in simple terminology, for example, "God is for us."

The lists of words and phrases of the long sentences are prominent. When I analyze the passage in advanced study at a later time, I will want to spend much time over these precious truths.

Punctuation. Question marks are prominent in the second and third paragraphs. (I count seven.) Paul gives answers to all the questions he raises, either directly or indirectly.

TONE OF THE SEGMENT

The atmosphere is one of assurance and triumph in hardships and spiritual conflict. Key phrases that set such a tone are "we know" (v. 28), "we overwhelmingly conquer" (v. 37), "I am convinced" (v. 38).

FOCUS ON THE FULL TEXT

I would do for each of the three paragraphs what was demonstrated in the preceding example, the analytical reading of a *paragraph* (John 4:39-42).

Phrases. I will mark in my Bible some prominent phrases that stand out to me as I read the paragraphs again.

8:28-30 The prominent repeated phrases are these: "whom He . . . , these He . . ."

8:31-34 A repeated construction involves indentifi-cations:
"God is the one who . . ."
"Christ Jesus is He who . . ."

8:35-39 The lists are prominent here, the many parts of which are kept together by the small words *or* (v. 35) and *nor* (vv. 38-39).

Pauses.

1) At the end of the first paragraph I pause long in my reading, to reflect on the deep doctrines I have just read.

2) I don't pause very long at the end of the second paragraph, because its overall theme continues into the next paragraph.

3) The two questions of verse 35 are the last ones. I pause after them (together with the parenthesis of verse 36), to introduce the triumphant an-swers of verses 37-39.

Inflections.

1) The key to effective reading (silent or audible) of this segment is what I do with the many ques-tions.

2) The phrases of assurance ("I am convinced")
   must be read with conviction and finality.

3) I read verse 36 as a sideline parenthesis.

4) As I read the last two verses of the passage, I am
   climbing higher and higher. Each word of this
   phrase is emphatic: "nor any other created
   thing." The remainder of verse 39 is the climax.

Emphases and relationships. I recall some emphasized and related things that I've already seen, and look
for others that I may show on a talking text.

Emphases:

1) Repeated words: "love," "Who," "nor"

2) Other key words: "know," "convinced," "for
   us," "give," "separate," "conquer," "called"

Relationships:

1) The lists of the first and third paragraphs

2) The intimate spiritual relationship between God
   and believers

3) The pervading theme: "God is for us"
   For example:

GOD IS FOR US

- no break down   8:28-30
- no charges   8:31-34
- no separation   8:35-39

Talking Text of Romans 8:28-39 (NASB)

GOD IS FOR US
28 And **we know** that
      GOD causes all things
                to work together **for good**
      to those (1) WHO LOVE GOD,
      to those (2) WHO ARE CALLED
                according to **His purpose.**
29 For WHOM He FOREKNEW,
      He also PREDESTINED
      to become **conformed** to the image of His Son,
                that He might be

the first-born among many brethren;
30 and WHOM He PREDESTINED,
    these He also CALLED;
and WHOM He CALLED,
    these He also JUSTIFIED;
and WHOM HE JUSTIFIED,
    these He also GLORIFIED.

NO BREAKDOWN

31 What then shall we say to these things?
        If GOD IS FOR US,
        who is against us?
32 He who
    (1) did not spare His own Son,
    but
    (2) delivered Him up for us all,
    how will He not also
            with Him
            freely give us all things?
33 Who will bring a CHARGE against GOD'S ELECT?
    ———→ God is the one who justifies;
34 and who is the one who CONDEMNS?
    ———→ CHRIST JESUS is He who
        (1) died,
        (2) yes, rather who was raised,
        (3) who is at the right hand of God,
        (4) who also intercedes for us.

NO CHARGES

35 Who shall separate us
            from the LOVE of CHRIST?
    Shall tribulation, or distress, or persecution,
        or famine, or nakedness,
            or peril, or sword?
36 Just as it is written,
    "For Thy sake we are being put to death
        all day long;   [Ps. 44:22]
    We were considered as SHEEP
                    to be SLAUGHTERED."
37 But in all these things
    we
        OVERWHELMINGLY CONQUER
        THROUGH HIM
                who loved us.
38 For I am convinced that
    neither death, nor life,
        nor angels, nor principalities,
        nor things present, nor things to come,
        nor powers,
39   nor height, nor depth.
        nor any other created thing,
        shall be able
            to separate us
            from the LOVE of GOD,
                which is in CHRIST JESUS OUR LORD.

NO SEPARATION

Fig. 4:12

I record the text on paper as a textual recreation, showing these and other emphases and relationships as they come to me.

Theme of the passage. The title shown on the talking text suggests this theme: "God is for the believers—those who love Him are called by Him."

Applications. The applications of a full passage like this are legion. Here are a few:

1) Because I love God and am called by Him, I can rest assured that He will work all things for my good.
2) I should *want* to live pleasing to God, since He has predestined me to be conformed to His Son's likeness.
3) In God's sight, I am righteous through the death of Christ, so no one can bring a charge against me.
4) No one and nothing can separate me from the love of Christ and from the love of God.

5

The Activities of Informational Reading ▬,▬,▬,

Every passage of Scripture is important because it is an integral part of the inspired whole. Whether a passage is read devotionally, analytically, or for factual information, the reading should serve the divine purposes for which it was written. Of the three kinds of reading, the devotional and analytical approaches are the ones most often used. Sometimes a passage even calls for all three kinds of reading. The purpose of this chapter is to see what is involved in informational reading and how it can help the Christian learn all that God wants him to know.

I. What Informational Reading Is

We describe informational reading as:

1) Any reading not classified as devotional or analytical (though the latter two do provide information as well)
2) Usually very factual, with a minimum of devotional or analytical potential (e.g., the list of warriors recorded in Numbers 1:20-46)

Among the objectives of informational reading are:

1) To inform the reader (or listener) of facts and truths
2) To complement the surrounding Bible text, such as by illustrating or providing an example
3) To give setting, or to complete an account
4) To emphasize one main point, by way of *quantity* of text

Most passages of the Bible that are for informational reading concern history, reporting hosts of facts, small and large. It should not surprise us that so much of the Bible is history. Since God is the Creator and Ruler of the universe, history in the broad sense is the sequence of all events, recorded or unrecorded, *in relation to God*. In a very real sense, any history book that accurately records historical facts involving individuals and groups of individuals (race, nation, alliance, etc.) contributes to a knowledge of God, disclosing such things as His permissive will or efficient will. If so-called "secular" history books contribute to a knowledge of God, how much more should the biblical historical books have to offer in this respect! Surely such books as Genesis were written to describe, even for the generations of their first reading, the ways of man (basically sinful) and the ways of God (holy, just, gracious, long-suffering, and so on). Of course, even in the so-called historical books there are those sections that were intended to do more than give description or example, such as the recording of the Decalogue (Exodus 20) and Levitical laws (Leviticus) to be incorporated in the very worship of the people of God.

Since so much of the Bible is factual in nature, involving, in addition to history, such areas of knowledge as geography, culture, psychology, and nature, it is vital that the reader be alert to ways he can do his informational reading in an effective way and fulfill the objective taught in 2 Timothy 3:16-17. The suggestions and examples in this chapter are intended to help.

II. Getting Things Ready

A. PRELIMINARY CHECKS

Make all the preliminary checks described earlier, to prepare yourself for the reading of the passage. More is said here about a few of those checks.

TYPE Since some passages call for all three kinds of reading—devotional, analytical, informational—you can expect to find informational reading in any part of the Bible, for example: as poetry, prophecy, prayer, narrative, historical fact, biography, autobiography, testimony, parable, doctrine, apocalypes (with many symbols).

BEF , AFT It is very important for informational reading that you check the surrounding passages. After you have looked before and after, you should be able to answer the question, "Why was this passage included in the Bible text?"

B. TEXT LAID OUT: THE STRUCTURE

The passage of informational reading is usually long, especially if it is historical. The format of the text in your Bible will probably show the beginning and end of the segment, and how it is divided into paragraphs. For example, refer to the first chapter of Numbers in your Bible. Observe the paragraph pattern beginning at verse 20. A segment could be 1:20-46, with paragraph divisions as shown in the Bible. Also scan verses 1-19. Do you observe why this passage is more for informational reading than it is for devotional or analytical reading? So Numbers 1 has two segments for informational reading.

C. TONE

Usually a passage for informational reading has one main thought running through it, with one main atmosphere, if any.

III. Focus on the Full Text

Below are some things you should do as you focus on the full text in informational reading.

1) Recall the setting you observed in the preliminary checks.
2) Read the passage again. Be alert to strong, colorful words and key words, which sometimes get lost in the many routine details of an informational passage.
3) Look for emphases and relationships. These will usually be prominent in a passage whose structure is symmetrical, like Numbers 1:20-46.
4) Try to identify the segment's main subject or theme by one word.
5) Record your impressions of the passage.
6) What does the passage contribute to this part of the Bible book? (See the objectives of informational reading in chapter 1).
7) Think about applications, since "all Scripture is . . . profitable" (2 Timothy 3:16). This is where all Bible reading should lead.

IV. Further Study

Sometimes an informational reading of a passage will suggest that more be done with it at a later time, involving analytical study and even devotional reading.

V. Occasional Reading

Occasional reading, which could be classified as a type of informational reading, is a kind of public reading that is done for special occasions such as weddings, funerals, graduations, dedications, baptisms, inaugurations, commissions, and holidays. The Bible has excellent passages that are directed to these moments. When the Scriptures are read aloud, it is very important that the reader communicate with his listeners clearly and interpretatively. He who has a deep, heartfelt love of Scripture will do that best. J. Edward Lantz says, "An effective reader of God's Word must love it, study it, and understand it as fully as possible."[1]

VI. Informational Reading of an Old Testament Segment ⸚⸗⸚⸗⸚⸗

Exodus 39:22-31 (NIV)

Other Priestly Garments

²²They made the robe of the ephod entirely of blue cloth—the work of a weaver— ²³with an opening in the center of the robe like the opening of a collar,ᵃ and a band around this opening, so that it would not tear. ²⁴They made pomegranates of blue, purple and scarlet yarn and finely twisted linen around the hem of the robe. ²⁵And they made bells of pure gold and attached them around the hem between the pomegranates. ²⁶The bells and pomegranates alternated around the hem of the robe to be worn for ministering, as the LORD commanded Moses.

²⁷For Aaron and his sons, they made tunics of fine linen—the work of a weaver— ²⁸and the turban of fine linen, the linen headbands and the undergarments of finely twisted linen. ²⁹The sash was of finely twisted linen and blue, purple and scarlet yarn—the work of an embroiderer—as the LORD commanded Moses.

³⁰They made the plate, the sacred diadem, out of pure gold and engraved on it, like an inscription on a seal: HOLY TO THE LORD. ³¹Then they fastened a blue cord to it to attach it to the turban, as the LORD commanded Moses.

ᵃ23 The meaning of the Hebrew for this word is uncertain.

Fig. 5.1

PRELIMINARY CHECKS

BOOK   The book is Exodus, the second of five books of the Law.

TYPE   The type of writing is prose narrative.

1. J. Edward Lantz, *Reading the Bible Aloud* (New York: Macmillan, 1959), p. xii.

SETTING   Exodus is the story of God's people Israel in Egypt (chapters 1-12); on their journey to Mount Sinai (13-18); and receiving God's instructions at Sinai (19-40).

PASSAGE   The passage I have chosen for the informational reading is one segment, Exodus 39:22-31. This segment can be broken down into three paragraphs: 22-26; 27-29; 30-31.

MN   There is only one footnote to this NIV passage. It is about the word "collar" (v. 23): "The meaning of the Hebrew for this word is uncertain."

QU   There are references to the Lord's instructions to Moses ("as the Lord commanded Moses"), but no quotes. Words of an inscription on the sacred diadem are printed: "HOLY TO THE LORD" (v. 30).

BEF   The preceding paragraphs of chapter 39 describe the specifications for other things to be made for the services of the Tabernacle.

AFT   The very next verse is the bright conclusion to the description of things made: "So all the work on the tabernacle, the tent of meeting, was completed. The Israelites did everything just as the Lord commanded Moses" (39:32).

CON   This passage is the conclusion of the section "Items Made," as shown in this outline:

TABERNACLE:

ITEMS MADE	36:8—39:31
INSPECTION	39:32-43

TEXT LAID OUT

Segment. NIV labels this segment at *Other Priestly Garments.*

Paragraphs. NIV shows new paragraphs at verses 22, 27, and 30. These paragraph divisions are natural:

1) At or near the opening of each paragraph is the phrase, "They made."
2) Each paragraph concludes with the phrase, "as the Lord commanded Moses."
3) Each paragraph describes different things made—for example, the first paragraph is about the *robe.*

Sentences. The sentences are of moderate length and similar composition.

Phrases, words. The most obvious feature of the phrases and words is the variety of color and pieces of garments that make up the text.

Punctuation. Three enclosing sets of dashes appear in the NIV translation: "—the work of a weaver—" (vv. 22, 27) and "—the work of an embroiderer—" (v. 29).

TONE

Atmosphere is not prominent here, unless one visualizes the bustling activity of the craftsmen's work areas.

FOCUS ON THE TEXT

Key words and phrases:

1) "as the Lord commanded Moses"—At the conclusion of each paragraph.
2) "HOLY TO THE LORD"—This is the most prominent phrase of the passage.

Strong, colorful words: "they made," "pure gold," "fine linen," "sacred diadem" "work."

Emphases:

1) different references to doing the work
2) The repetition of "as the Lord commanded Moses" is prominent.

Relationships: The prominent relationship is between the *doing* and the Lord's *command.*

Main theme. The craftsmen did their work, just as the Lord commanded Moses.

My impressions: God must like beauty and detail, as well as function.

Contribution to the narrative of Exodus: God was teaching His people to be obedient in all things. This is one example of the book that demonstrates how craftsmen and leader Moses were obedient followers of the Lord.

Applications:

1) I should give the best of my time, devotion, and energy to the Lord.
2) The Lord wants me to obey Him in all things.
3) My devotion should reflect this motto: HOLY TO THE LORD.

FURTHER STUDY

I may want to refer to a Bible encyclopedia and commentaries to learn more about the clothing, materials, and colors that made up the priestly garments. My curiosity and interest are heightened when I consider that these items must be of importance in God's sight, for Him to have them recorded in His book.

More Old Testament passages than New Testament passages call for informational reading. This is partly because the New Testament is, for the most part, the compact, substantive fulfillment or climax of the long detailed narratives, messages, and prophecies of the Old Testament. Most New Testament passages are read either for devotions or analysis.

VI. Informational Reading of a New Testament Segment ¯,¯,¯,

Revelation 8:13—9:12 (NASB)

13 And I looked, and I heard ¹an eagle flying in ᵃmidheaven, saying with a loud voice, "ᵇWoe, woe, woe, to ᶜthose who dwell on the earth; because of the remaining blasts of the trumpet of the ᵈthree angels who are about to sound!"

13 ¹Lit., *one eagle*
ᵃRev. 14:6; 19:17 ᵇRev. 9:12; 11:14; 12:12 ᶜRev. 3:10 ᵈRev. 8:2

CHAPTER 9

AND the ᵃfifth angel sounded, and I saw a ᵇstar from heaven which had fallen to the earth; and the ᶜkey of the ¹ᵈbottomless pit was given to him.
   2 And he opened the ¹bottomless pit; and ᵃsmoke went up out of the pit, like the smoke of a great furnace; and ᵇthe sun and the air were darkened by the smoke of the pit.
   3 And out of the smoke came forth ᵃlocusts ¹upon the earth; and power was given them, as the ᵇscorpions of the earth have power.
   4 And they were told that they should not ᵃhurt the ᵇgrass of the earth, nor any green thing, nor any tree, but only the men who do not have the ᶜseal of God on their foreheads.
   5 And ¹they were not permitted to kill ²anyone, but to torment for ᵃfive months; and their torment was like the torment of a ᵇscorpion when it ³stings a man.
   6 And in those days ᵃmen will seek death and will not find it; and they will long to die and death flees from them.
   7 And the ¹ᵃappearance of the locusts was like horses prepared for battle; and on their heads, as it were, crowns like gold, and their faces were like the faces of men.
   8 And they had hair like the hair of women, and their ᵃteeth were like *the teeth* of lions.
   9 And they had breastplates like breastplates of iron; and the ᵃsound of their wings was like the sound of chariots, of many horses rushing to battle.
   10 And they have tails like ᵃscorpions, and stings; and in their ᵇtails is their power to hurt men for ᶜfive months.
   11 They have as king over them, the angel of the ᵃabyss; his name in ᵇHebrew is ¹ᶜAbaddon, and in the Greek he has the name ²Apollyon.
   12 ᵃThe first Woe is past; behold, two Woes are still coming after these things.

1 ¹Lit., *shaft of the abyss*
ᵃRev. 8:2 ᵇRev. 8:10 ᶜRev. 1:18 ᵈLuke 8:31; Rev. 9:2, 11

2 ¹Note v. 1
ᵃGen. 19:28; Ex. 19:18 ᵇJoel 2:2, 10

3 ¹Lit., *into*
ᵃRev. 9:7; Ex. 10:12-15 ᵇRev. 9:5, 10; 2 Chr. 10:11, 14; Ezek. 2:6

4 ᵃRev. 6:6 ᵇRev. 8:7 ᶜRev. 7:2, 3

5 ¹Lit., *it was given to them* ²Lit., *them* ¹Lit., *strikes*
ᵃRev. 9:10 ᵇRev. 9:3, 10; 2 Chr. 10:11, 14; Ezek. 2:6

6 ¹Job 3:21; 7:15; Jer. 8:3; Rev. 6:16

7 ¹Lit., *appearances*
ᵃJoel 2:4

8 ᵃJoel 1:6

9 ᵃJoel 2:5; Jer. 47:3

10 ᵃRev. 8:3, 5; 2 Chr. 10:11, 14; Ezek. 2:6 ᵇRev. 9:19 ᶜRev. 9:5

11 ¹Or, *Destruction* ²Or, *Destroyer*
ᵃLuke 8:31; Rev. 9:1, 2 ᵇRev. 16:16; John 5:2 ᶜJob 26:6; 28:22 marg., 31:12 marg.; Ps. 88:11 marg.; Prov. 15:11

12 ᵃRev. 8:13; 11:14

Fig. 5.2

PRELIMINARY CHECKS

┌─────────┐
│ BOOK   │ The book is Revelation, the last book of the
└─────────┘
Bible.

TYPE   The type of writing is apocalyptic, which is prophetic disclosure of last times, using figurative language and many visions and symbols.

PASSAGE   The passage is Revelation 8:13—9:12. This passage records the fifth of the trumpet judgments of the book of Revelation. (The top of the NASB page identifies this subject.) The passage is the length of one segment.

MN   There are various marginal notes in the NASB. The most helpful ones are: the translations *Destruction* for *Abaddon* and *Destroyer* for *Apollyon* (v. 11).

QU   There are no Old Testament quotes in the segment.

BEF   The preceding paragraphs of 8:6-12 record the first four trumpet judgments.

AFT   The remainder of chapter 9 records the sixth trumpet judgment.

CON   The continuity is very apparent: our passage is in the middle of the descriptions of the trumpet judgments.

TEXT LAID OUT

Segment. The Layman's Bible Study Notebook shows 8:13—9:12 to be a segment for study.

Paragraphs. The segment breaks down into four paragraphs, the first and last being just the length of one verse:

8:13—three woes are introduced
9:1-6—the activities of the fifth-trumpet locusts

> 9:7-11—the appearances of the fifth-trumpet lo-
>   custs
> 9:12—conclusion: "The first woe is past"

Sentences. The average length of the sentences is three lines. The opening verse (8:13) is the longest; the closing verse (9:12) is the shortest.

Phrases, words. Most of the strong words are short and sharp (e.g., "woe, "kill," "sting").

Some words and phrases serve as attention getters, e.g., "woe," "behold," "still coming."

TONE

The tone is one of torment and agony—people seeking death but not finding it.

FOCUS ON THE TEXT

Key words and phrases. "Woe," "torment," "bottom-less pit," "seal of God," "long to die," "five months."

Strong, colorful words. "Smoke," "locusts," "scorpi-on," "sting," "king over them."

Emphases. The agony of the locust judgments, and its unceasing quality.

The first and last verses emphasize the character of "woe." The exclamation point at the end of 8:13 accen-tuates this.

Relationships. The judgments are described in var-ious ways. I note the many descriptions of verses 7-10, with the repeated word "like."

Main theme. The fifth trumpet brings agonizing torment, not death.

My impressions. The many pictures of torment are God's way of saying why the judgments for sin should be feared and avoided.

Contribution to revelation. This is one of many prophecies of judgments to come in the last days.

Applications:

1) I should fear the God of judgment and the judgments of God.
2) I should never forget that God's judgments are for sin.
3) Some judgments go on for a *long* time.
4) God makes a way of escaping the judgments, before they come.

Conclusion

What one book would you take with you to your "desert island," to read for the remainder of your days? Would it be the Bible? If so, can you visualize reading it in the three different ways that we have discussed in this book?

One last thought: Do you recall the earmarks of a "truly great book" identified by authors Adler and Van Doren?

1) It is inexhaustible.
2) You see new things each time you read it.
3) It will always remain above you.
4) It will keep on lifting you till you die.
5) It will help you to grow.

If you are a devoted Bible reader, your response surely is that no book comes near the Bible for fulfilling these descriptions of a truly great book. Take time now to read Psalm 119 with one purpose in mind: to catch the fervor and conviction of the psalmist for the blessedness of having The Book of God.

Appendix 1:

Identification of Segment Divisions of Six Bible Books

The segment unit is the most frequently used unit for Bible reading and study, especially because of its substantive and practical length. Following is a list of suggested segment units for six books of the Bible. An abridged survey chart of each of the books is also given for the purpose of orientation, as well as to justify some segment divisions that do not concur with chapter divisions.

MARK

PROCLAMATION				WHO AM I?	PASSION		
1:1	4:1	6:1	7:1	8:27	8:31	9:30	11:1
POPULARITY & OPPOSITION	WORDS & WORKS	NAZARETH	OVER THE BORDER	CRISIS POINT	CRISIS WEEK	TO JERUSALEM	PASSION WEEK

1:1-13	6:1-13; 14-29	11:1-19; 20-33
14-34	6:30-44; 45-56	12:1-27
35-45	7:1-23	28-44
2:1-17	24-37	13:1-23
2:18—3:6	8:1-26	24-37

3:7-19a	8:27—9:1	14:1-25
19b-35	9:2-13; 14-29	26-52
4:1-20	9:30-42; 43-50	53-72
21-41	10:1-16	15:1-21
5:1-20	17-31; 32-45	22-47
21-43	46-52	16:1-20

JOHN

PUBLIC MINISTRY: SIGNS WROUGHT		PRIVATE MINISTRY: SELF REVEALED			
1	5	12:36b	18	20	21
ANNOUNCEMENT	ELABORATION & CONFLICT	DISCOURSE & PRAYER	CRUCIFIXION	RESURRECTION	

1:1-18	7:1-24	13:1-20
19-39	25-52	21-38
40-51	7:53—8:11	14:1-31
2:1-12; 13-25	8:12-30	15:1-11
3:1-21	31-59	12-27
22-36	9:1-12	16:1-16
4:1-26	13-34; 35-41	17-33
27-42	10:1-21	17:1-26
43-54	10:22-42	18:1-27
5:1-18	11:1-16	28-40
19-29	17-44	19:1-22
30-47	45-53; 54-57	23-42
6:1-21	12:1-22	20:1-18
22-40	23-36a	19-31
41-51	36b-50	21:1-14
52-71		15-23; (24, 25)

I JOHN

GOD IS LIGHT	GOD IS LOVE	
1	3	5
"IF WE WALK IN LIGHT"	"WE HAVE FELLOWSHIP ONE WITH ANOTHER"	

1:1-10	3:1-24
2:1-17	4:1-21
18-29	5:1-12; 13:21

PSALMS

(No topical sequence, though each book has been compared with those of Pentateuch)				
1	42	73	90	106 150
BOOK I	BOOK II	BOOK III	BOOK IV	BOOK V

The majority of the chapters of the Psalms are of segment length. The following list, representing the longer Psalms, presents recommended units of study for these Psalms.

18:1-19	69:1-18	105:1-11
20-30	19-36	12-36
31-50	71:1-16	37-45
22:1-18; 19:31	17-24	106:1-15
31:1-18	78:1-20	16-39
19-24	21-39	40-48
35:1-18	40-55	107:1-22
19-28	56-72	23-43
37:1-17	89:1-18	109:1-19
18-29	19-37	20-31
30-40	38-52	118:1-14
44:1-8	102:1-17; 18-28	15-29
9-26	104:1-23	119: (each 8 verses)
68:1-20	24-35	139:1-18; 19-24
21-35		

NEHEMIAH

REBUILDING THE WALLS			RELIGIOUS REFORMS		
1	3	7	8	11	12:27 13
PLAN AND PREPARATION	CONSTRUCTION	CENSUS	RENEWAL of CONVENANT	PEOPLE SURVEY	DEDICATION

1:1-11	7:1-73a	11:1-36
2:1-20	7:73b—8:18	12:1-30
3:1-32	9:1-5	31-47
4:1-23	6-31	13:1-14
5:1-19	32-38	15-31
6:1-19	10:1-39	

ISAIAH

HOLINESS	RIGHTEOUSNESS		JUSTICE	ORIGINS of GRACE	WORKINGS of GRACE	GLORIES of GRACE	
1	13	24	36	40	49	60	66
EXHORTATIONS & WARNINGS	PROPHECIES RE SURROUNDING NATIONS	PROMISES AND WOES	CAPTIVITY	DELIVERANCE—FUTURE GLORIES			

1:1-9	24:1-23	9-20
10-20	25:1-12	21-28
21-31	26:1-21	45:1-13
2:1-21	27:1-13	14-25
2:22—3:15	28:1-13	46:1-13
3:16—4:1	14-29	47:1-15
4:2-6	29:1-12	48:1-16
5:1-17	13-24	17-22
18-30	30:1-18	49:1-13
6:1-13	19-33	14-26
7:1-25	31:1-9	50:1-11
8:1-22	32:1-20	51:1-11
9:1-21	33:1-12	12-23
10:1-19	13-24	52:1-15
20-34	34:1-17	53:1-12
11:1-16	35:1-10	54:1-17
12:1-6	36:1-22	55:1-13
13:1-22	37:1-20	56:1-12
14:1-21	21-38	57:1-21
22-32	38:1-22	58:1-14
15:1-9	39:1-8	59:1-21
16:1-14	40:1-11	60:1-22
17:1-14	12-31	61:1-11
18:1-7	41:1-13	62:1-12
19:1-17	14-29	63:1-19
18-25	42:1-9	64:1-12
20:1-6	10-25	65:1-16
21:1-17	43:1-13	17-25
22:1-25	14-28	66:1-14
23:1-18	44:1-8	15-24

Appendix 2:

Selected List of Prominent Subjects of the Bible

Below are listed some prominent subjects of the various books of the Bible, and the passages in which they appear. When you scan the Bible text of each passage, you will be able to decide what kind of reading you would use for that passage.

Old Testament

Genesis
1:1—2:3	Creation
3:1—4:26	Fall of Man
6:1—9:29	Flood

Exodus
12:1-28	Passover
13:1—15:21	Red Sea Deliverance
15:22—18:27	Wilderness Journey
chapter 20	Ten Commandments
25:1—31:18	Tabernacle Specifications
32:1—34:35	Idolatry at Sinai

Leviticus
    1:1—7:38   Five Offerings
    chapters 8-10; 21-22   Priesthood
    chapter 16   Day of Atonement
    chapters 23-25   Holy Times

Numbers
    chapters 1, 26   Census

Deuteronomy
    31:1—34:12   Moses' Parting Words

Joshua
    13:1—21:45   Land Allocations

Judges
    3:7—16:31   Judges of Israel

2 Samuel
    11:1—20:26   David's Troubles

1 Kings
    5:1—9:9   Solomon's Temple
    16:29—19:21   Elijah

2 Kings
    1:1—8:15   Elisha
    25:1-16   Fall of Jerusalem

1 Chronicles
    1:1—9:44   Genealogies
    10:1-19   Split of the Kingdom

Ezra
    1:1—6:22   Restoration

Nehemiah
    chapters 3-6   Building Projects

Esther
    4:1—10:3   Jews Spared

Psalms
    78, 105, 106, 136   History
    51   Penitential
    20-24   Messianic
    8, 19, 29, 33, 65, 104 Nature

Isaiah
    chapter 6   Isaiah's Call

Ezekiel
    37:1-10   Vision of Dry Bones

Daniel
    9:1-27   Seventy Weeks

New Testament

Matthew
    1:1-17   Genealogy of Christ
    5:3—7:27   Sermon on the Mount
    13:1-53   Kingdom Parables
    24:1—25:46   Olivet Discourse

Mark
    4:35—6:32   Miracles
    9:2-13   Jesus' Transfiguration

Luke
    2:1-20   Christmas Story

John
    1:1-18   Prologue
    3:1-21   Nicodemus

17:1-26	High-priestly Prayer
20:1-31	Resurrection

Acts
2:1-47	Church Is Born
9:1-19a	Saul Saved
13:1—21:17	Missionary Journeys

Romans
3:21—5:21	Justification
9:1—11:36	Israel

1 Corinthians
7:1-40	Marriage
11:2—14:40	Spiritual Gifts
15:1-58	Resurrection Body

2 Corinthians
8:1—9:15	Christian Giving

Galatians
3:1—5:1	Faith and Law

Ephesians
6:10-18	Christian's Armor

Philippians
2:5-11	Christ's Emptying

Colossians
2:4—3:4	Heresies Exposed

1 Thessalonians
4:13-18	Jesus' Return

2 Thessalonians
    2:1-17   Antichrist

1 Timothy
    3:1-13   Church Officers

2 Timothy
    4:1-22   Paul's Farewell

Titus
    1:1-16   False Teaching

Hebrews
    4:14—10:18   Christ the High Priest

James
    1:1-18   Faith and Trials

1 Peter
    3:13—5:11   Suffering and Trial

2 Peter
    3:7-10   World's Physical Dissolution

1 John
    1:1—2:2   Fellowship
    2:8-29   Antichrists

Revelation
    2:1—3:22   Letters to Seven Churches
    19:1—20:15   Final Judgment

Appendix 3:

Selected List of Sixty-Six Golden Verses in the Bible[1] (one from each book of the Bible)

Genesis 3:15. First Messianic promise.

Exodus 12:13. Life insurance.

Leviticus 25:10. The Year of Jubilee.

Numbers 9:17. The pilgrim's guide.

Deuteronomy 29:29. The secret things.

Joshua 1:8. The price of success.

Judges 16:20. The lost power.

Ruth 1:16. A shining example of constancy.

I Samuel 15:22. The indispensable virtue.

II Samuel 18:33. The father's lament.

I Kings 3:9. The prayer for wisdom.

II Kings 6:17. The divine reinforcements.

I Chronicles 4:10. A wonderful prayer in dark surroundings.

II Chronicles 16:9. The all-seeing eye.

Ezra 7:10. The faithful scribe.

Nehemiah 4:17. A true labor union.

Esther 4:14. The woman for an emergency.

Job 42:10. An enriching prayer.

Psalm 84:11. The matchless Giver.

Proverbs 3:15. The precious possession.

1. From *The New Chain-Reference Bible* (Indianapolis: B. B. Kirkbride, 1934), p. 288. Used by permission.

Ecclesiastes 12:13. The great conclusion.

Song of Solomon 1:6. The unfaithful vineyard keeper.

Isaiah 9:6. The most wonderful child.

Jeremiah 29:13. The greatest discovery.

Lamentations 3:22. God's unfailing mercies.

Ezekiel 33:32. The sentimental hearers.

Daniel 6:10. The unchangeable habit of prayer.

Hosea 6:3. The road to divine blessing.

Joel 2:28. The outpouring of the Spirit.

Amos 8:11. The spiritual famine.

Obadiah 4. The humbling of the proud.

Jonah 1:3. An expensive journey.

Micah 6:8. Practical religion.

Nahum 2:4. Nothing new under the sun.

Habakkuk 2:14. World-wide missions.

Zephaniah 2:3. Seeking the Lord.

Haggai 2:4. A ringing call to duty.

Zechariah 4:6. The true means of success.

Malachi 3:10. The tither's promise.

Matthew 7:7. The three-fold promise.

Mark 16:15. The great commission.

Luke 10:20. The real reason for joy.

John 15:7. The master-key of prayer.

Acts 1:8. The watchword of the spiritual campaign.

Romans 10:9. The plan of salvation.

I Corinthians 3:11. The only foundation.

II Corinthians 4:6. The illuminated heart.

Galatians 2:20. Dying to live.

Ephesians 4:13. The highest development.

Philippians 2:5. The mind of Christ.

Colossians 3:1. The heavenly ambition.

I Thessalonians 5:23. Entire sanctification

II Thessalonians 3:10. The duty to labor.

I Timothy 4:12. The young man's example.

II Timothy 2:4. The soldier's separation.

Titus 2:14. The Redeemer's purpose.

Philemon 15. A tender appeal.

Hebrews 11:13. The pilgrims' vision.

James 5:20. The soul-winner's achievement.
I Peter 1:18, 19. The cost of redemption.
II Peter 1:21. The origin of prophecy.
I John 3:2. The sons of God.
II John 6. Love and obedience.
III John 4. The minister's joy.
Jude 24, 25. The divine keeper.
Revelation 11:15. The consummation of the divine plan.

Appendix 4:

This Old Testament history chart will help you place an Old Testament book in its original historical setting. For example, if you are reading a passage of Jeremiah, the chart will tell you that Jeremiah was prophesying at that time to the southern kingdom of Judah, just before the Jews were taken into captivity in Babylon.

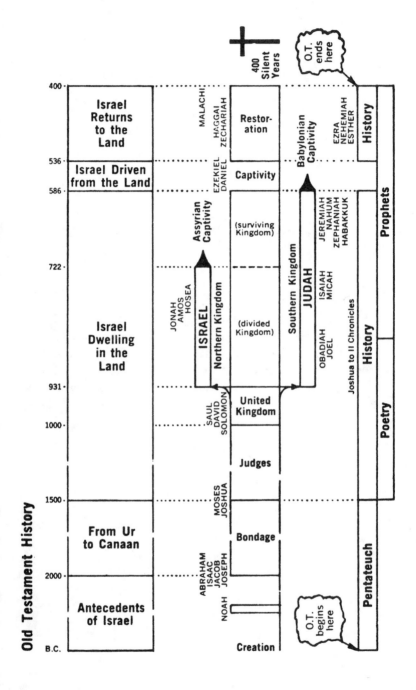

Old Testament History

Appendix 5:

READING THROUGH THE BIBLE IN 3 YEARS

	FIRST YEAR	SECOND YEAR	THIRD YEAR
JAN.	MARK	PSALMS 42-72	I and II KINGS
FEB.	GENESIS	ROMANS & HEBREWS	PSALMS 107-150
MAR.		ECCLESIASTES	JEREMIAH–LAMENTATIONS
		NUMBERS	
APR.	ACTS	JOB	EZRA–NEHEMIAH–ESTHER
			SONG of SOLOMON
MAY		GALATIANS to COLOSSIANS	I and II CHRONICLES
JUNE	EXODUS	DEUTERONOMY	HOSEA to MALACHI
JUL.	PSALMS 1-41	I PETER to III JOHN	JAMES, JUDE, PHILEMON
AUG.	MATTHEW	PSALMS 73-106	ISAIAH
SEP.	LEVITICUS	JOHN	
OCT.	PROVERBS	JOSHUA	I TIM.–TITUS–II TIM.
		JUDGES–RUTH	
NOV.	EZEKIEL–DANIEL	CORINTHIANS–THESSALONIANS	LUKE
DEC.	REVELATION	I and II SAMUEL	

The above sequence has been arranged with topical order and variety in mind. As you begin each new book, determine the length of each daily reading, according to the time-span allotted.

Appendix 6:

Readings of Romans 15:1-4 in Ten Versions*

1. *New King James Version*

15 We then who are strong ought to bear with the scruples of the weak, and not to please ourselves.

² Let each of us please *his* neighbor for *his* good, leading to edification.

³ For even Christ did not please Himself; but as it is written, *"The reproaches of those who reproached You fell on Me."*

⁴ For whatever things were written before were written for our learning, that we through the patience and comfort of the Scriptures might have hope.

2. *New American Standard Bible*

CHAPTER 15

NOW we who are strong ought to bear the weaknesses of ªthose without strength and not *just* please ourselves.

*The order moves from the most literal (1) to the most paraphrastic (10).

2 Let each of us ^aplease his neighbor ¹for his good, to his ^bedification.

3 For even ^aChrist did not please Himself; but as it is written "^bTHE REPROACHES OF THOSE WHO REPROACHED THEE FELL UPON ME."

4 For ^awhatever was written in earlier times was written for our instruction, that through perseverance and the encouragement of the Scriptures we might have hope.

3. *Revised Standard Version*

15 We who are strong ought to bear with the failings of the weak, and not to please ourselves; ² let each of us please his neighbor for his good, to edify him. ³ For Christ did not please himself; but, as it is written, "The reproaches of those who reproached thee fell on me." ⁴ For whatever was written in former days was written for our instruction, that by steadfastness and by the encouragement of the scriptures we might have hope.

4. *New Berkeley Version in Modern English*
   (Modern Language Bible)

15 WE WHO ARE STRONG OUGHT TO bear with the scruples of those who are weak. We should not please ourselves. ²But each of us should please his neighbor for his welfare, to strengthen him. ³For even Christ did not please Himself but, as it is written,^p "The reproaches of those who reproached you fell on me."

⁴All those writings of long ago were written for our instruction, so that through the patience and encouragement of the Scriptures we might have hope.

5. *New International Version*

15 We who are strong ought to bear with the failings of the weak and not to please ourselves. [2]Each of us should please his neighbor for his good, to build him up. [3]For even Christ did not please himself but, as it is written: "The insults of those who insult you have fallen on me."[a] [4]For everything that was written in the past was written to teach us, so that through endurance and the encouragement of the Scriptures we might have hope.

6. *Today's English Version (Good News for Modern Man)*

15 We who are strong in the faith ought to help the weak to carry their burdens. We should not please ourselves. [2] Instead, we should all please our brothers for their own good, in order to build them up in the faith. [3] For Christ did not please himself. Instead, as the scripture says, "The insults which are hurled at you have fallen on me." [4] Everything written in the Scriptures was written to teach us, in order that we might have hope through the patience and encouragement which the Scriptures give us.

7. *New English Bible*

15 Those of us who have a robust conscience must accept as our own burden the tender scruples of weaker men, and not consider ourselves. Each of us must consider his neighbour and think what is for his good and will build up the common life. For Christ too did not consider himself, but might have said, in the words of Scripture, 'The reproaches of those who reproached thee fell upon me.' For all the ancient scriptures were written for our own instruction, in order that through the encouragement they give us we may maintain our hope with fortitude.

8. *Jerusalem Bible* (Roman Catholic)

15 We who are strong have a duty [1] to put up the qualms of the weak without thinking of ourselves. • Each of [2] us should think of his neighbours and help them to become stronger Christians. • Christ did not think of himself: the words [3] of scripture—*the insults of those who insult you fall on me*—apply to him. • And indeed [4] everything that was written long ago in the scriptures was meant to teach us something about hope from the examples scripture gives of how people who did not give up were helped by God.

9. *New Testament in Modern English* (Phillips)

15.1

We who have strong faith ought to shoulder the burden of the doubts and qualms of others and not just to go our own sweet way. Our actions should mean the good of others— should help them to build up their characters. For even Christ did not choose his own pleasure, but as it is written:

The reproaches of them that reproached thee fell upon me.

For all those words which were written long ago are meant to teach us today; that when we read in the scriptures of the endurance of men and of all the help that God gave them in those days, we may be encouraged to go on hoping in our own time.

10. *The Living Bible*

15 EVEN IF WE believe that it makes no difference to the Lord whether we do these things, still we cannot just go ahead and do them to please ourselves; for we must bear the "burden" of being considerate of the doubts and fears of others—of those who feel these things are wrong. Let's please the other fellow, not ourselves, and do what is for his good and thuse build him up in the Lord. ³ Christ didn't please himself. As the Psalmist said, "He came for the very purpose of suffering under the insults of those who were against the Lord." ⁴ These things that were written in the Scriptures so long ago are to teach us patience and to encourage us, so that we will look forward expectantly to the time when God will conquer sin and death.

Selected Bibliography

Adler, Mortimer J., and Van Doren, Charles. *How to Read a Book* (rev. ed.). New York: Simon and Schuster, 1972.

Fee, Gordon D., and Stuart, Douglas. *How to Read the Bible for All Its Worth*. Grand Rapids: Zondervan, 1982.

Fischer, James A. *How to Read the Bible*. Englewood Cliffs, N.J.: Prentice-Hall, 1981.

Goldingay, John. *Reading the Bible for the First Time*. Valley Forge: Judson, 1979.

Jensen, Irving L. *Enjoy Your Bible*. Chicago: Moody, 1969.

———. *Independent Bible Study*. Chicago: Moody, 1963.

———. *Jensen's Survey of the New Testament*. Chicago: Moody, 1981.

———. *Jensen's Survey of the Old Testament*. Chicago: Moody, 1978.

———. *Layman's Bible Study Notebook*. Eugene, Oreg.: Harvest House, 1978.

———. *Mark* (Do-It-Yourself Bible Study guide). San Bernardino: Here's Life, 1983.

Lantz, J. Edward. *Reading the Bible Aloud*. New York: Macmillan, 1959.

Leedy, Paul D. *Improve Your Reading*. New York: McGraw-Hill, 1956.

Richards, I. A. *How to Read a Page*. Boston: Beacon Press, 1942.

Sire, James W. *How to Read Slowly*. Downers Grove, Ill.: InterVarsity, 1978.

Sproul, R. C. *Knowing Scripture*. Downers Grove, Ill.: InterVarsity, 1977.

Sterrett, T. Norton. *How to Understand Your Bible*. Downers Grove, Ill.: InterVarsity, 1974.

Stott, John R. W. *Understanding the Bible*. Glendale, Calif.: Regal, 1972.

Thomas, Geoffrey. *Reading the Bible*. Carlisle, Pa.: Banner of Truth, 1980.